EXTEN
SCIENC

ASTRONOMY

Selected Topics

Bernard Abrams
Patrick Moore

Stanley Thornes (Publishers) Ltd

First published in 1989 by
Stanley Thornes (Publishers) Ltd
Old Station Drive
Leckhampton
CHELTENHAM GL53 0DN
England

*An exception is made for the puzzles on pp. 32, 98 and 108. Teachers may photocopy a puzzle to save time for a pupil who would otherwise need to copy from his/her copy of the book. Teachers wishing to make multiple copies of a word puzzle for distribution to a class without individual copies of the book must apply to the publishers in the normal way.

British Library Cataloguing in Publication Data

Abrams, Bernard
  Astronomy.
  1. Astronomy
  I. Title   II. Moore, Patrick   III. Series
  520

  ISBN 0-85950-938-9

Typeset by Tech-Set, Gateshead, Tyne & Wear.
Printed and bound in Great Britain by Ebenezer Baylis & Son, Worcester.

CONTENTS

Chapter 4 Planets, comets and meteors

Chapter 5 The stars

Chapter 6 The Galaxy

Chapter 7   The distant universe

Chapter 8   The celestial sphere

Chapter 9   Images from space

Chapter 10 **Space flight**

Colour plates (between pp. 56 and 57)

PREFACE

Astronomy is the oldest science. It has a fascination and beauty which attract more interest today than ever; we are fortunate to be living through one of the most active periods in the history of astronomical research. The exploration of the Solar System is under way, and powerful new telescopes will soon be probing the depths of the universe from Earth and from space.

Incorporating all branches of science, astronomy is also one of the most stimulating subjects for study in the classroom. In writing this book we have tried to produce an up-to-date account which tackles many of the questions posed by enquiring young minds.

To follow the work in this book it is not necessary to have access to a powerful telescope. However, any observations which can be made will be very useful – but remember, you must *not* look directly at the Sun, with or without a telescope.

Eight of the chapters are arranged in two parts. How far each topic is studied will depend on the course being followed. Suggestions for project work and questions to check pupils' understanding are included.

Teachers will note that the material is arranged in a logical sequence, but this order need not be strictly followed. The first part of a chapter (all of Chapter 10) contains an introduction to the topic, which is extended in the second part (all of Chapter 8) to a level appropriate to a first examination option in physics or full examination course in astronomy. The colour plates should be used where appropriate to illuminate descriptions and explanations in the text. At the end of chapters there are some suggestions for projects, and a selection of questions – these include some word puzzles together with more challenging problems. A list of sources of visual aids, further reading and astronomical data can be found in the Appendices on pp. 124–6.

We hope that teachers and their pupils will find this book both useful and enjoyable.

Bernard Abrams (*Cheltenham College*)
Patrick Moore (*Selsey*)
1989

ACKNOWLEDGEMENTS

The authors would like to thank Paul Doherty for his excellent illustrations.

The authors and publishers are grateful to the following who gave permission for their photographs to be reproduced:

National Aeronautics and Space Administration (NASA) (cover, pp. 44, 120; Plates 1, 2, 5, 6, 7, 8, 9, 10, 11)
The Observatories of the Carnegie Institution of Washington (pp. 20, 46, 78, 84)
Dan Turton (p. 35 (left))
Andy Packer (pp. 35 (right), 73, 75 (upper), 101)
Dr. Vehrenberg KG (p. 36; Plate 16)
Anglo-Australian Telescope Board (p. 75 (lower))
John Fletcher (p. 77 (upper))
Royal Observatory, Edinburgh (p. 80, © Royal Observatory, Edinburgh; Plates 13, 14, 18, © Royal Observatory, Edinburgh and Anglo-Australian Telescope Board)
Ron Arbour (p. 91)
National Optical Astronomy Observatories (NOAO) (p. 106)
Max Planck Institut für Aeronomie, Stuttgart (p. 107 (right))
Mount Wilson Observatory (Plate 3)
US Naval Research Laboratory (Plate 4)
Gina Watkins-Capen (Plate 12)
California Institute of Technology (Plates 15, 17 © California Institute of Technology 1959).

THE EARTH

CENTRE OF THE UNIVERSE?

For many thousands of years, the sight of the Sun, Moon and stars moving round the skies convinced mankind that the Earth (Plate 1) was the centre of the universe. Some bright objects in the sky 'wandered' from time to time and earned the name *planet* (which means wanderer) but their complicated movements were explained away and this Earth-centred view survived from before the time of Ptolemy (second century AD) until Nicolaus Copernicus placed the Sun at the centre of the *Solar System* in 1543. From then onwards, the Earth's status as one of the planets circling the Sun became established – slowly. Religious objections persisted, and the *Ptolemaic view* (Figure 1.1(a)) was slow to disappear. For some time after Copernicus it was dangerous to support his opinions openly – imprisonment (or worse) could result. Even so, by the end of the seventeenth century the *Copernican theory* was widely accepted.

Figure 1.1

In Ptolemy's theory the Earth is at the centre (a), while the Copernican view placed the Sun at the centre and relegated the Earth to a less important position; (b) the modern view of Earth and its satellite

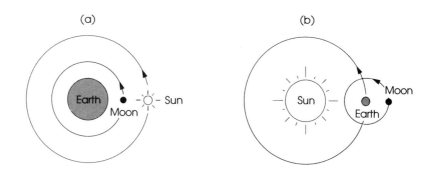

THE MOVING EARTH

We cannot sense directly that the Earth is moving in space, which is partly why the idea of a stationary Earth at the centre of the universe seemed right. But we are moving – Earth spins round once in nearly 24 hours, making the Sun and stars rise and set, and giving day and night. Also, the Earth completes one circuit round the Sun (an *orbit*) in $365\frac{1}{4}$

Figure 1.2

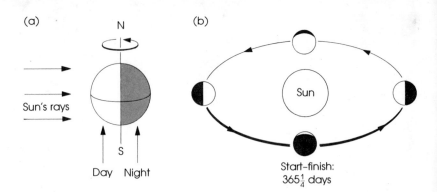

(a)

N

Sun's rays

S

Day   Night

(b)

Sun

Start–finish:
$365\frac{1}{4}$ days

days or 1 year (Figure 1.2). Our planet's average distance from the Sun is 149 600 000 kilometres (93 000 000 miles), which astronomers call an *astronomical unit*.

GRAVITY

The Earth is held in orbit round the Sun by the force of *gravity*. Through this force, *all* objects are attracted to each other, but the effects only become easily noticeable when one object has the mass of something like a small planet. The idea of a universal law of gravitation is supposed to have occurred to Sir Isaac Newton (1642–1727) when he saw an apple fall from a tree. The action of being pulled towards the ground is how we experience gravity.

SEASONS

During summer in the northern hemisphere, the Earth is slightly further away from the Sun than it is in winter. The seasonal change in climate must, therefore, have another cause – it results from the tilt of the Earth's axis, which is inclined at $23\frac{1}{2}$ degrees as shown in Figure 1.3.

The Sun reaches a higher point in the sky each day during summer and this results in longer periods of daylight and shorter nights than in winter. When the Sun remains low near the horizon, as in winter, its rays travel through a thicker portion of the Earth's atmosphere before reaching the ground and lose much of their warming effect (Figure 1.3(b)).

THE ATMOSPHERE

The layer of gases which surround the Earth is called the *atmosphere*. It is composed largely of nitrogen (78%) and oxygen (21%), with traces of carbon dioxide, water vapour

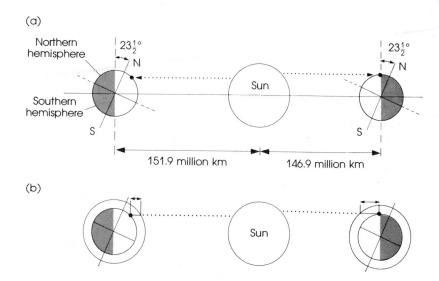

(a)

Northern hemisphere

Southern hemisphere

$23\frac{1}{2}°$ N

$23\frac{1}{2}°$ N

Sun

S

S

151.9 million km

146.9 million km

(b)

Sun

Figure 1.3

Although the Earth is slightly further away from the Sun during summer than it is in winter in the northern hemisphere, the tilt of the Earth's axis turns the northern hemisphere towards the Sun

and other substances. Further out into space, the 'edge' of the atmosphere is found at approximately 750 kilometres – but there is not a sharp cut-off at this point; rather, the density of the atmospheric gases gradually tails away.

ACTIVITY 1

Demonstration: Why is the sky blue?

The teacher will need: a glass or plastic fish tank, water supply, instant milk, soluble blue ink, a torch, a stirrer, a darkened room.

The sky may be blue due to something in the air being coloured blue. To test this, some blue ink can be added to a tank of water, and a torch shone through. What is the appearance of the torch (the Sun) and the ink solution (the sky) as viewed through the tank? Is this model accurate?

The exercise can be repeated using fresh water to which one pint of instant milk has been added. What is the appearance of the torch (Sun) and milk solution (sky) now? What is there in air which could have the same effect as the milk powder?

Our bright sky is a consequence of scattering of sunlight by the atmosphere. Blue light is scattered more efficiently than other colours, giving us a blue sky which 'drowns' the light from stars in daytime.

Erosion

Complex motions in the atmosphere produce weather systems. Clouds form as water evaporates from the oceans, wind and rain combine to produce violent storms. The action of wind and rain causes erosion on the surface of the Earth, changing the landscape constantly. Activity within the Earth (volcanic action, for example) is also responsible for large-scale changes over long periods of time. As a result of these activities, many of the craters which formed on Earth in the distant past have disappeared. One notable exception is Meteor Crater in Arizona, caused by a large lump of rock falling from space. The crater has survived for over 20 000 years and is just over 1 kilometre across.

PLANET EARTH

The Earth is an almost perfectly spherical planet. It has an equatorial diameter of 12 756 kilometres (7926 miles) and a polar diameter of 12 714 kilometres (7900 miles). This tangerine shape is caused by the Earth's rotation, which makes the equator bulge (Figure 1.4).

Figure 1.4

The spinning of the Earth causes an equatorial bulge of over 40 kilometres

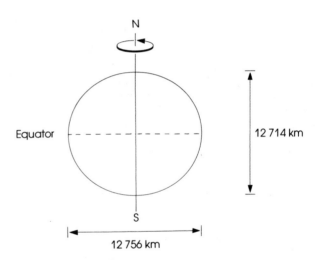

Underneath the atmosphere, most of Earth's surface is covered by water – only 30% is land. Beneath the solid surface *crust* (only about 10 kilometres thick in some areas) is a molten *mantle*. Material from the mantle which reaches the surface during volcanic eruptions is known as lava. Deeper within the Earth temperatures continue to rise, and the *core* itself may reach 5000 degrees Celsius.

The core, which contains iron, gives the Earth a magnetic field like that of a bar magnet.

A useful aid to navigation, the magnetic field is closely aligned to the Earth's axis of rotation, but is subject to slow changes and has undergone complete north–south reversals in the past at approximately 200 000 year intervals.

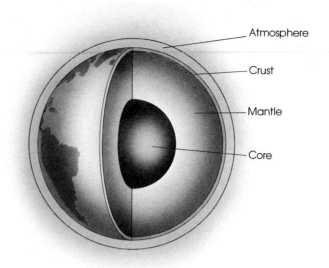

Figure 1.5

Structure of the Earth

Atmosphere

Crust

Mantle

Core

Figure 1.6

Compass needles align themselves with the Earth's magnetic field which is like that of a bar magnet

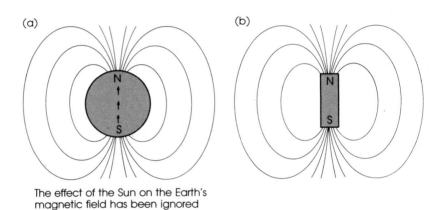

(a)

(b)

The effect of the Sun on the Earth's magnetic field has been ignored

ACTIVITY 2

Magnetic fields

You will need: a bar magnet, paper or card, iron filings.

Place the bar magnet underneath the paper and sprinkle on top some iron filings. *Gently* flick the edge of the paper and note the pattern of the filings. Compare this with Figure 1.6.

Summary of Earth data

Average distance from Sun	149 600 000 kilometres (93 000 000 miles)
Orbital period	$365\frac{1}{4}$ days
Length of 1 day	24 hours
Mass	6 million million million million kilograms
Equatorial diameter	12 756 kilometres
Average density	5.52 grams per cubic centimetre
Surface gravity	9.8 newtons per kilogram

THE AGE OF THE EARTH

The origin and age of the Earth have puzzled scientists for many years, and various ideas have emerged.

After a careful study of ages quoted in the Bible, Archbishop Ussher of Armagh concluded in the 1650s that the Earth was created on 26 October 4004 BC. A more scientific estimate by the nineteenth century physicist Lord Kelvin suggested that the Earth had cooled to its present state over a period of around 30 million years. Even this estimate of the Earth's age is extremely low compared to the currently accepted value of 4700 million years obtained from radioactive dating of rocks.

The question of how the Earth (and other members of the Solar System) was formed remains the subject of debate. Although most astronomers accept that the Sun and planets formed from a swirling, contracting cloud of gas and dust in space (Figure 1.7), the theory leaves some details unexplained.

Figure 1.7

Formation of the Earth together with other members of the Solar System from a cloud of gas and dust (the 'solar nebula')

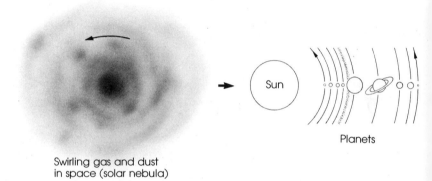

Swirling gas and dust in space (solar nebula)

Planets

Although no planets have yet been identified for certain orbiting other stars, it is likely that there are *many* other planets.

LIFE ON EARTH

The existence of life on Earth makes our planet truly unique – as far as we can know. How did it arise?

Very early in the history of the Earth, the surface was molten. Prevailing conditions just after the surface solidified were much too extreme for living things to survive – high temperatures, no liquid water and an atmosphere containing not oxygen, but suffocating gases. Only after the Earth had cooled sufficiently for water vapour to condense and remain as a liquid could there be any possibility of life developing. Earth's distance from the relatively constant Sun, its mass and rotation rate combined to produce the right surface conditions. The energy from electrical storms and ultraviolet rays from the Sun probably caused vital chemical reactions in the primitive atmosphere which deposited new molecules into the oceans. From these compounds, life developed.

The oxygen in our atmosphere began to accumulate when some simple plant-like cells started using water and the gas carbon dioxide to produce their food. The presence of oxygen, a by-product of this process, led to a wider variety of life which evolved over hundreds of millions of years to give the complex organisms we see today.

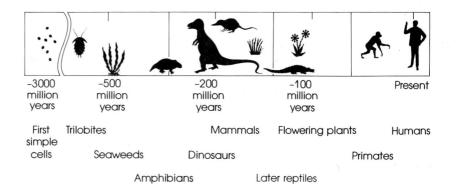

Figure 1.8

The emergence of life on Earth

-3000 million years	-500 million years	-200 million years	-100 million years	Present

First simple cells Trilobites   Mammals   Flowering plants   Humans

Seaweeds   Dinosaurs   Primates

Amphibians   Later reptiles

SUGGESTION FOR A PROJECT

1 Find out about the damage which aerosol gases called 'CFCs' are causing to the atmosphere.

QUESTIONS

1 What is an astronomical unit?

2 Using Figure 1.3 on page 3, explain why Australia (in the southern hemisphere) experiences summer while Britain is in winter.

3 Why do we have a leap year every 4 years?

4 What extra problems would face developing life on Earth if our planet was:
(a) much closer to the Sun
(b) much smaller and much less massive
(c) spinning very slowly, say one rotation every 100 days.

5 Do you think it likely that life exists on another planet somewhere in space? What are your reasons?

THE STRUCTURE OF THE ATMOSPHERE

If you throw an object into the air (a cricket ball, for example) it will rise to a certain height and then fall down. If you give it a greater starting speed, it will rise higher. If you could give it a starting speed of 11 kilometres (7 miles) per second, it would never come down at all, because the Earth's gravity would not be strong enough to draw it back, and the ball would escape into space (Figure 1.9). This is why 11 kilometres per second is known as the Earth's *escape velocity*.

Figure 1.9

The velocity of a projectile determines whether it will escape into space, enter orbit, or fall back to Earth

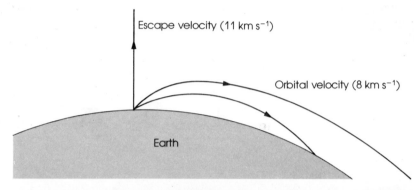

Figure 1.10

Layers of the atmosphere

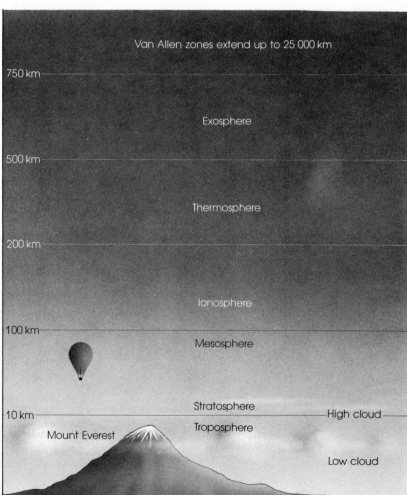

The air we breathe is made up of millions upon millions of particles, all moving around at high speeds. Fortunately for us, the particles cannot travel as fast as 11 kilometres per second, and so the Earth can hold on to its atmosphere. If the escape velocity were much less (as it is, for example, with the Moon), the atmosphere would escape, and the Earth would be an airless, lifeless world.

The atmosphere is divided into several layers, though of course there is no sharp boundary between them (Figure 1.10). The bottom 11 kilometres (7 miles) is called the troposphere, and is where we live; even at the top of the troposphere the air has become too thin for us to breathe. Next comes the stratosphere, which extends up to about 50 kilometres (30 miles). Above the stratosphere come other regions, and in one of them, the ionosphere, we find a layer which reflects radio waves back to Earth (Figure 1.11) and makes long-range radio communication possible.

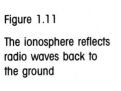

Figure 1.11

The ionosphere reflects radio waves back to the ground

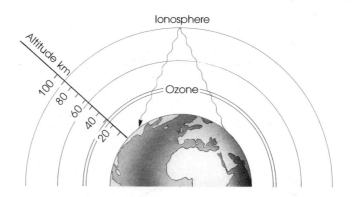

The atmosphere also protects us from dangerous short-wave radiations from space; this is because of a layer of ozone, which is a special form of oxygen, extending between 25 and 40 kilometres (15 and 25 miles) above the Earth's surface.

In 1958 the first successful American artificial satellite, *Explorer 1*, discovered that there are zones of radiation high above the Earth. These are known as the Van Allen zones, in honour of Dr James Van Allen, who designed the equipment carried in *Explorer 1*, One zone lies between 500 and 1000 kilometres (300 to 600 miles) and the other between 15 000 and 25 000 kilometres (9000 and 15 000 miles). The zones are made up of electrically charged particles trapped in the Earth's magnetic field. If the zones become 'overloaded' by collecting extra particles sent out by the Sun, particles stream down into upper air, and produce the lovely glows which we call aurorae or polar lights. Aurorae are best seen in high latitudes, because the particles are attracted to the Earth's magnetic poles.

THE MOVING CONTINENTS

The Earth's lands and seas have not always had the same shapes as they do now. It seems that in the distant past all the continents were joined together in one huge landmass (Figure 1.12) and have gradually drifted apart; you can see how the coast of South America fits quite neatly into the outline of Africa. The continents are still moving very slowly in relation to each other and the Earth's crust is divided up into what we call *plates*. The constant movement results in the building up of mountains, while the boundaries between plates are often marked by volcanoes.

Figure 1.12

How the landmasses were once joined together

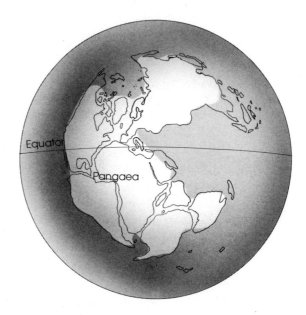

Volcanoes

A volcano arises over a 'hot spot' in the Earth's mantle. As the landmasses shift, the volcano moves away from the hot spot and becomes dead or *extinct* (Figure 1.13). Thus in the Hawaiian Islands, the massive volcano Mauna Kea has left the hot spot; it has not erupted for thousands of years, and will probably never do so again (which is lucky, as a major astronomical observatory has been built on top of it). On the other hand, the neighbouring volcano Mauna Loa is still very active.

Figure 1.13

How a volcano moves away from a hot spot

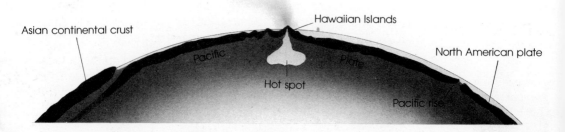

EARTH'S ORBIT

It is usually thought that the Earth moves round the Sun in a circular orbit, but this is not quite true; the orbit is an *ellipse* (Figure 1.14). At our nearest to the Sun (*perihelion*) we are 147 000 000 kilometres (91 300 000 miles) away; at our furthest (*aphelion*) 152 000 000 kilometres (94 400 000 miles). In the early seventeenth century, the German mathematician Johannes Kepler found that a planet moves fastest when closest to the Sun, and slowest when furthest away; this means that the Earth moves at its greatest velocity near perihelion, in December of each year (see p. 54).

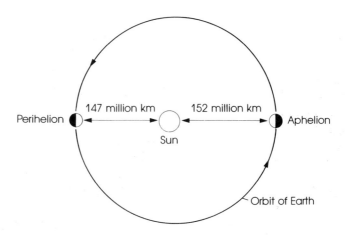

Figure 1.14

The elliptical orbit of the Earth

Because the Earth takes one year to go round the Sun, the Sun seems to go right round the sky in the same period. Of course, we cannot see stars in the daytime, because the sky is too bright, but we can work out where the Sun must lie against the starry background. The apparent yearly path of the Sun against the stars is known as the *ecliptic*.

With respect to the stars, the Sun seems to move eastward by about one degree per day. (One degree is 1/360 of a circle.) This means that although the Earth's true 'day' is 23 hours 56 minutes 4.1 seconds long (in astronomy this may be shown as $23^h 56^m 4^s.1$), the mean solar day is slightly longer.

DAYLIGHT AND DARKNESS

We know that the Earth's equator divides the world into two hemispheres, north and south. In the same way, the equator of the sky divides the celestial sphere into two hemispheres. In a northward direction, the Earth's axis of rotation points to a position closely marked by a fairly bright star, Polaris or the Pole Star; unfortunately the south pole of the sky is marked only by a much fainter star (see p. 94).

The Sun does not move round the sky along the celestial equator. During northern summer, when the Sun is moving north of the celestial equator, daylight in the northern hemisphere is longer than the period of night, and at the North Pole of the Earth, the Sun remains above the horizon for six months. During this time, the South Pole is in darkness. When the Sun is moving south of the celestial equator, the situation is reversed (Figure 1.15).

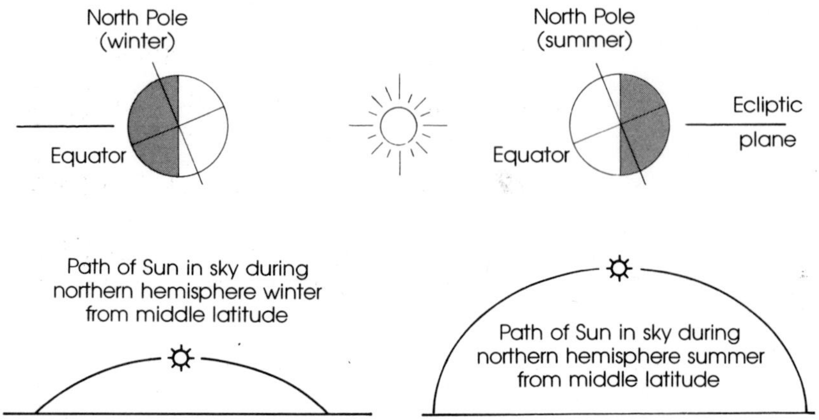

North Pole (winter)

North Pole (summer)

Ecliptic plane

Equator

Equator

Figure 1.15

The apparent path of the Sun across the sky in summer and winter

Path of Sun in sky during northern hemisphere winter from middle latitude

Path of Sun in sky during northern hemisphere summer from middle latitude

Time zones

The 'day' is not exactly 24 hours long, as we have seen, but in everyday life we divide it into 24 hours for the sake of convenience. Astronomers always use GMT or Greenwich Mean Time, which begins at midnight (0 hours); thus 8 p.m. is 20.00 hours GMT. The world has been divided into 'time zones'. For example, the civil time in Sydney, Australia, is ten hours ahead of GMT; Cape Town is two hours ahead, New York five hours behind, and so on. Remember this if you want to make a telephone call to a friend in New York. If you ring him from London at eight o'clock in the morning, you will wake him up, because it will be only three o'clock in the morning by New York time!

GMT, known astronomically as Universal Time (UT), can be used to calculate the local mean time (LMT) elsewhere, given the relevant longitude. For example, when it is 10.00 UT in London, the local time in Sydney (longitude 150°E) is 20.00 hours, as one hour corresponds to 15° in longitude (180° per 12 hours). Similarly in San Francisco (120°W) the local time is 02.00 hours, eight hours behind UT in London. As it would lead to unworkable complexities if the time 'changed' every few degrees of longitude, time zones such as those described above have been introduced to rationalise the situation.

6 What is meant by escape velocity – and why is the escape velocity of the Earth so important to us?

7 In what way do we depend upon the atmosphere for our existence, apart from the fact that we have to have air to breathe?

8 What are aurorae, and how are they caused? If you want to see them, would you go to north Norway, Italy, or the Sahara Desert?

9 In Hawaii, why is the volcano of Mauna Kea extinct, while Mauna Loa still erupts?

10 What is meant by the ecliptic?

11 Why is a solar day slightly longer than a true day, as measured using the stars?

12 When it is 11.00 hours UT in London, what is the local mean time in
(a) Memphis (90°W) (b) Kiev (30°E)
(c) Rawalpindi (75°E)

CHAPTER 2

THE MOON

THE SURFACE OF THE MOON

Even with the naked eye, you can see bright regions and darker patches on the Moon. Use binoculars, or a telescope, and you will see a tremendous amount of detail. The large dark plains are known as 'seas', though there has never been any water in them. There are also mountains, peaks, valleys and vast numbers of the walled circular formations that we usually call craters. The Moon is indeed a rugged world.

THE SEAS

The seas or *maria* cover much of the Moon. We still use the romantic names given to them by the early telescopic astronomers, who believed them to be water-filled; thus we have the Mare Imbrium (Sea of Showers), Mare Tranquillitatis (Sea of Tranquillity), Oceanus Procellarum (Ocean of Storms), Sinus Iridum (Bay of Rainbows) and so on. In general the Latin names are used in preference to the English equivalents.

A photograph of the Moon's surface is shown in Figure 2.4 (p. 20). Because the same hemisphere is always turned towards us, the seas and other features always appear in virtually the same positions on the disc.

The seas are smoother than the uplands, though they contain many craters. They are large; the most extensive of them, the rather irregular Oceanus Procellarum, has an area greater than that of the Mediterranean Sea. Some of the regular seas are mountain-bordered. Part of the border of the Mare Imbrium is formed by the Lunar Apennines and the Lunar Alps, with peaks in some places to over 5000 metres.

CRATERS

The walled formations which are generally known as craters are found all over the Moon. Often they are named after famous scientists of the past, and they range from vast enclosures hundreds of kilometres across down to tiny pits too small to be seen at all from Earth. A typical large crater has a wall which rises to a moderate height above the outer surface. The floor is sunken, and there may be a central mountain or mountain group. Though the walls may rise to hundreds of metres, a crater is not deep in relation to its width, and in profile is more like a shallow saucer than a steep-sided mine shaft (Figure 2.1).

Figure 2.1

The profile of a typical crater on the Moon

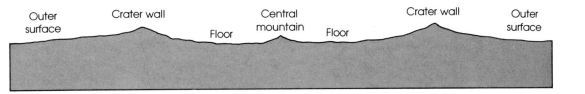

Most of the large crater formations are circular, but they often break into each other and deform each other. When this happens, it is almost always the smaller formation which breaks into the larger.

Some craters, such as Tycho in the southern highlands and Copernicus in the Mare Nubium (Sea of Clouds) are the centres of systems of bright streaks or rays. These rays are surface deposits, and are visible only when the Sun is high over them; near Full Moon they are so conspicuous that they tend to hide all the other features.

Most astronomers believe that the craters were formed by bodies which bombarded the Moon in the remote past, though others believe that many of them are of volcanic origin. In any case, they are very ancient by everyday standards. Nothing much has happened on the Moon for at least two thousand million years, though there are occasional reports of mild emissions of gas from below the surface.

OBSERVING THE MOON

There are various minor features on the Moon's surface, such as the valleys; the domes, which are low, rounded swellings; the chains of craterlets; and the crack-like features known as rills, rilles or clefts. Many of these can be seen with a small telescope, but the appearance of the Moon alters from night to night, because of the changing angle of the Sun's rays.

To see a crater at its best, look for it when it is near the *terminator*, or boundary between the day and night hemispheres. The crater floor will then be partially or completely filled with shadow (Figure 2.2(a)). When the crater is further away from the terminator there will be less shadow (Figure 2.2(b)) and when the Sun is high over the crater there will be almost no shadow at all, so that the formation may be hard to identify unless it has a very dark floor or very bright walls. This means that Full Moon is the very worst time to start finding your way around the lunar surface. Far better views will be had when the Moon is a crescent, half or gibbous shape (see Phases).

Figure 2.2

Craters are best seen near the terminator, where they are illuminated at an angle

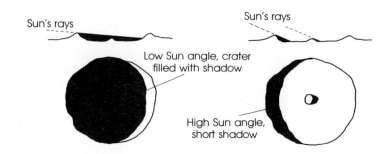

PHASES

The Moon has no light of its own. It shines only by reflecting the light of the Sun, and this is why the Moon shows regular *phases* as it waxes and wanes.

In Figure 2.3 (which is not to scale) the Moon is shown at four positions. As the Sun can light up only one half of the Moon at any one time, one side 'shines' while the other is dark. The lunar phase at any instant depends on the extent of our view of the sunlit half.

Figure 2.3

Phases of the Moon

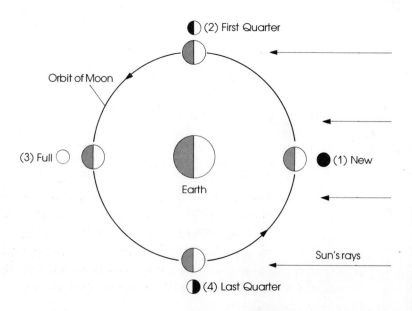

At *New Moon* (position 1) the dark or night side is turned towards us, and we cannot see the Moon at all – unless it passes exactly between the Earth and the Sun, blotting out the Sun briefly and producing a solar eclipse (see Chapter 3).

As the Moon moves along its orbit, a little of the 'day' side starts to be turned in our direction. The Moon becomes visible as a thin *crescent* in the night sky, and the phase slowly increases until it reaches *First Quarter* (position 2). This term is rather confusing as we see a 'half' Moon at this point. The label refers to the fact that the Moon has completed one quarter of its orbit. It then moves on in this orbit, becoming a three-quarter or *gibbous* shape. At position 3 the whole of the sunlit side is facing us and the Moon is *Full*. It then becomes gibbous once more, returning to half at position 4 (*Last Quarter*) and finally another New Moon occurs at position 1.

ACTIVITY 3

Lunar phases

You will need: a darkened room, a torch and a white table tennis ball or polystyrene sphere. Work in threes.

To model the appearance of the Moon as it completes one orbit of the Earth, use the torch as a source of 'sunlight' and, with the small sphere representing the Moon, use the diagram below to act out the motions shown in Figure 2.3 and so see how the *lunar phases* arise. The torch-bearer should be more distant from the 'Earth' than is the 'Moon'. Each Person 'A' takes turns to follow the 'Moon'; he or she should note how much of the 'Moon's' disc is illuminated at each point. Change places so that each participant takes each role.

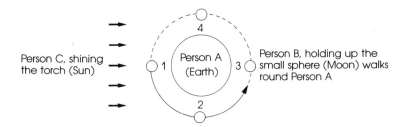

ECLIPSES OF THE MOON

It is likely that, in carrying out the lunar phases activity, you found that the 'Moon' entered the shadow of 'Earth' and became *eclipsed*. This is exactly what happens when an eclipse of the Moon occurs. Such an event is visible from an entire hemisphere on Earth, and lunar eclipses last for some time. For further information see p. 125.

ROCKETS TO THE MOON

The first successful rockets to the Moon were launched by the Soviet Union in 1959. It was one of these, *Luna 3*, which orbited the Moon and relayed the first pictures of the far side. The first men to reach the Moon were Neil Armstrong and Edwin Aldrin, in July 1969, from the lunar module of *Apollo 11*. Other flights followed, and a total of 12 men walked on the Moon; the last visit was by *Apollo 17* in 1972.

The Moon is not a friendly world. It has no air or water; the temperature at the equator is very high during the long lunar day, but bitterly cold at night as there is no atmosphere to blanket in the Sun's heat. Yet because the Moon is so close to us, there is no reason to doubt that permanent stations will be set up there in the fairly near future, and it is possible that some readers of this book will themselves go to the Moon.

SUGGESTIONS FOR PROJECTS

1 Take a tennis ball to represent the Earth, wrap string around it ten times, unravel the string and then put a table tennis ball on the far end to represent the Moon. This gives a rough idea of the scale of the Earth-Moon system.

2 Build a lunar crater, with raised walls and sunken floor. It can be of sand, plasticine, clay or papier mâché. Then use a torch to illuminate it from the side. Note how the shadow inside the crater changes as you raise or lower the torch.

3 Make a naked eye drawing of the Moon as accurately as you can, showing the dark 'seas'. Make sketches on different nights, to show how the appearance changes with the Moon's phase. If you have access to a telescope, repeat these observations for a selected area of the Moon's surface.

QUESTIONS

1 The crater Plato is circular, but as seen from Earth it looks oval. Why is this?

2 If you look at the Full Moon, you will see the Mare Crisium (Sea of Crises) near the edge of the disc. Will you ever be able to see it from Earth near the centre of the disc? Explain your answer.

3 Which is the best phase of the Moon for observing
(a) the bright ray systems?
(b) the craters?

4 Why does the Moon's surface become intensely cold during the lunar night?

5 If an Apollo mission takes 3 days to travel 400 000 kilometres to the Moon, what is its average speed in kilometres per hour?

6 Compete the following sentences by choosing the correct word from the list:

GIBBOUS   TERMINATOR   SHADOW
APOLLO   SATELLITE

(a) During a lunar eclipse the Moon enters the Earth's
_____.

(b) The American manned Moon missions were the
_____ series.

(c) Between First Quarter and Full, the Moon is
_____.

(d) The _____ is the boundary between day and night on the Moon.

(e) The Moon is the Earth's natural _____.

Apart from the Sun, the Moon is by far the most conspicuous object in the sky. This is not because it is large; it is much smaller than the Earth, and much less massive. Put the Earth in one pan of a gigantic pair of scales, and you would need 81 Moons to balance it. But on an astronomical scale our satellite is very close, and it stays together with us as we travel round the Sun. Fly ten times round the Earth and you will have covered a total distance greater than that between the Earth and the Moon. Data on our nearest neighbour are given below.

Summary of Moon data

Mean distance from Earth	376 284 kilometres (surface to surface)
	384 400 kilometres (centre to centre)
Revolution period (Earth orbit)	27.322 days
Axial rotation period	27.322 days
Synodic period (mean interval between successive new moons)	29 days 12 hours 44 minutes
Mean orbital velocity	3680 kilometres per hour
Diameter	3476 kilometres
Mass (Moon: Earth)	1:81
Escape velocity	2.38 kilometres per second

THE MARIA

The most prominent lunar features to the naked eye are the dark maria or 'seas'. A glance at Figure 2.4 reveals these maria, most of which are roughly circular in shape; even where overlap occurs, the individual shapes can be made out. A more detailed view will show that the maria are comparatively lacking in craters. Why is this?

The origin of the maria lies in the distant past and, many astronomers believe, is connected with impacts on the lunar surface. When the cataclysmic impacts on the Moon's surface began to decline just under four thousand million years ago, a number of large 'ring basins' had been excavated. Subsequently, lava seeped to the surface and flooded the ring basins, removing traces of old craters and creating the dark maria we see today. These maria are lightly cratered as their surfaces are much younger. If you had lived on Earth around two thousand million years ago, you would have seen a Moon very similar to the one visible today; its surface has changed little since that time.

Figure 2.4

The Moon, showing dark maria and bright cratered highlands

LUNAR ECLIPSES

The Earth casts a long shadow in space, as shown in Figure 2.5. If the (Full) Moon passes into the *umbra*, its supply of direct sunlight is cut off for a while, and the Moon turns a dim, often coppery colour until it comes out of the shadow again. This is a *lunar eclipse*. If the Moon remains in the *penumbra*, a slight dimming may be noticeable. Eclipses of the Moon may be either

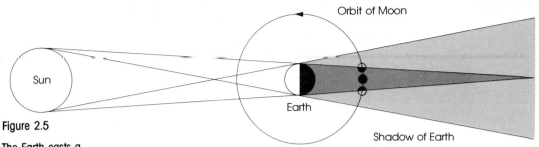

Orbit of Moon

Sun

Earth

Shadow of Earth

Figure 2.5

The Earth casts a
shadow far into space,
which the Moon
passes through during
a lunar eclipse

Figure 2.6

Some sunlight reaches
the Moon during a
total lunar eclipse due
to the effect of the
Earth's atmosphere

total or partial; they do not happen every month because on
most occasions the Moon passes either above or below the
Earth's shadow cone, avoiding eclipse.

During a total eclipse, some sunlight is bent on to the Moon's
surface by the Earth's atmosphere (Figure 2.6), so it remains
faintly visible.

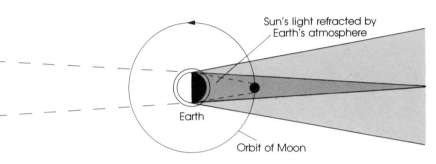

Sun's light refracted by
Earth's atmosphere

Sun

Earth

Orbit of Moon

THE AIRLESS MOON

It is not surprising to find that the Moon has no atmosphere.
The low escape velocity (2.38 kilometres per second) is not
enough to hold an atmosphere down, and any air the Moon may
once have had leaked away into space many millions of years
ago. The weak surface gravity also means that if you went to the
Moon, you would have only one sixth of your normal weight.

THE MOON'S ORIGIN

It was once thought that the Moon used to be part of the
Earth, and broke away, but this is not now believed to be the
case. The Moon and Earth may have always been separate bodies,
but they are of about the same age. Chemical differences suggest
that the Earth and Moon formed apart, with the Earth somehow
'capturing' the Moon at a later date.

However, the 'capture' event central to this theory has a low
probability of happening. Calculations on a powerful computer
suggest that it is possible for a collision between a large object
(with, say, 15% of the Earth's mass) and the very young Earth
to produce a Moon with the observed differences in
composition.

TIDES

Much of the Earth's surface is covered with water. The gravitational pull of the Moon causes the waters to rise and fall, creating *tides* (Figure 2.7). Although the Earth's surface is not *entirely* covered by the oceans, the diagram is easier to interpret if we imagine that it is. Note that two tides are raised, one opposite the Moon as expected, but with another on the far side of the Earth away from the Moon; this arises because the solid Earth itself is pulled towards the Moon.

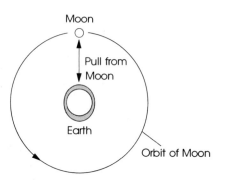

Figure 2.7

The tide-raising effect of the Moon's gravity

The Sun has a similar but smaller effect. However, when the Moon and Sun are pulling in the same direction, stronger tides (spring tides, nothing to do with the season) occur (Figure 2.8).

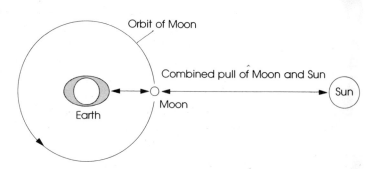

Figure 2.8

Spring tides occur when the Moon and Sun act together on the Earth's oceans

There is a further result of this tide-raising. As the Earth rotates, the tidal bulges are carried slightly out-of-line with the Moon. Friction between the solid Earth and the bulges is causing the Earth's rotation to slow down. Fossil records reveal that in the past there were nearer to 465 days in one year! In addition, the bulges themselves have an effect on the Moon, pulling it on in its orbit. As the Moon speeds up, so its distance from the Earth slowly increases – at a rate of just over 3 centimetres per year.

THE MOON'S ORBIT

The Moon's path is not a perfect circle. Like all celestial orbits, it is an ellipse, and the distance from Earth (centre to centre) ranges between 356 410 kilometres at its closest (*perigee*) out to 398 581 kilometres at its furthest (*apogee*).

Neither is it true to say simply that 'the Moon moves round the Earth'. To be accurate, the Earth and the Moon are moving together round their common centre of gravity, much as two bells of a dumb-bell will do if you twist them by the bar joining them (Figure 2.9). This 'balancing point' is called the *barycentre*. If the Earth and Moon were equal in mass, the barycentre would be midway between them; but the Earth is 81 times the more massive of the two, so that the barycentre actually lies well inside the Earth's globe.

Figure 2.9

The position of the barycentre in the Earth–Moon system

Earth
Moon
Barycentre

THE MOON'S ROTATION

The Moon's orbital period is exactly equal to the time that the Moon takes to spin once on its axis: 27.3 Earth days. This means that on the Moon, a period of sunlight is almost as long as two Earth weeks, while a lunar night is equally long. It also means that the Moon always keeps the same face turned towards the Earth.

If you walk round a chair, turning as you go so as to keep your face turned towards the chair, anyone sitting on the chair will never see the back of your neck. Yet when you have made one circuit, you will have completed a full turn on your 'axis', because you will have faced every wall of the room. This is how the Moon behaves with respect to the Earth. Note, however, that though the Moon keeps the same face turned towards the Earth, it does not keep the same face turned towards the Sun, so that day and night conditions are the same all over the surface of the Moon.

There is no mystery about this behaviour. We know that the Moon raises tides in our seas, and also in the Earth's solid globe, though the land tides are so slight that they are not noticeable. When the Moon was young, it was not solid, and the Earth raised powerful tides in its globe. As the Moon rotated, it had to fight against the Earth's pull, which was trying to keep a bulge turned earthward. The Moon's rotation was slowed down (rather as a spinning bicycle wheel will be slowed down by two brake shoes) until, relative to the Earth, the rotation had stopped.

Libration

We can, however, see a little more than 50% of the Moon's surface from Earth, though of course never more than 50% at any one time. The Moon spins on its axis at a constant rate, but it does not move round us at a steady speed, because its orbit is elliptical. Therefore, the position in orbit and the amount of spin become regularly 'out of step', and we can see a little more, first round one limb (edge) and then the other (Figure 2.10). This is the most important of the effects known as *librations*. At one time or another we can examine a total of 59% of the Moon's surface; the remaining 41% was unknown until the flight of the first rocket round the Moon, in 1959.

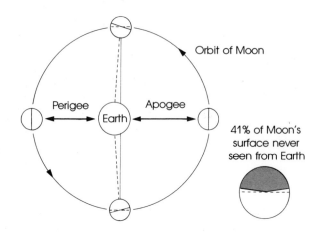

Figure 2.10

Libration allows us to see more than 50% of the lunar surface

QUESTIONS

7 What is the barycentre, and where is it?

8 When a total eclipse of the Moon occurs
(a) what is the phase of the Moon?
(b) why is the Moon still faintly visible?

9 Why does the Moon always keep the same face turned towards the Earth?

10 When the Moon appears to move in front of a star, would you expect the star's light to fade or cut off abruptly? Explain your answer.

11 If you weigh 600 newtons on Earth, what will you weigh on the Moon?

12 Neap tides (which are smaller than normal tides) occur when the effects of the Sun and Moon are working against each other. Draw a diagram to show how this happens.

13 Give *two* reasons why the full Earth will appear brighter in the Moon's sky, than the Full Moon will when seen from Earth.

THE SUN

The Sun is an object we all take for granted, except when it has not been seen for some time! It is 'ordinary' in the sense that it is very similar to many other stars in the night sky – for this is our Sun's identity, a rather average star which happens to have a family of planets in attendance.

The Sun is also unique in that it offers an intelligent civilisation on one planet the opportunity to study a star at exceptionally close quarters, while supplying all the energy they need to exist. Such study has revealed that the Sun is an enormous glowing sphere of gas, chiefly hydrogen (71%) and helium (27%). Some further information is given below.

Summary of Sun data

Mass	330 000 × Earth's mass (2 × 10^{30} kilograms)
Diameter	1 400 000 kilometres (865 000 miles)
Surface temperature	5500 degrees Celsius (5770 kelvins)
Core temperature	15 000 000 degrees Celsius
Mean distance from Earth	150 000 000 kilometres (93 000 000 miles = 1 AU)

On a simple level, studying the Sun can be very risky indeed. Direct observation, with or without filters, is at best dangerous and can lead to permanent blindness. Using a telescope or binoculars adds to the danger, and is best left to professional astronomers and experienced amateurs, with the exception of one method: *solar projection*.

Solar projection

You will need: access to a small telescope (refractor), white card, good weather.

In solar projection, an image of the Sun is projected onto a piece of white card shielded from direct sunlight by a shade screen placed around the telescope tube.

Locate the Sun by looking at the shadow of the telescope tube, *not* by sighting along the tube nor with a small 'finder' telescope which may be fitted to the main tube; this should be covered as it too will project the Sun's light and heat and can be dangerous.

Try to get the whole of the Sun's image onto the card (the distance from the card to the telescope must be found by experiment). Note the position of any *sunspots*, and try to follow them across the Sun's disc over the next few days. If a large spot is seen, does it have any structure?

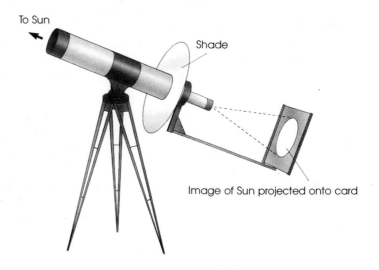

SUNSPOTS

Usually the Sun's disc will have a few sunspots (Plate 3), darker areas which may appear in groups. Their size can vary from those barely visible to complex spots with a diameter one eighth of the Sun's disc, corresponding to a range of 1 000 to 100 000 kilometres in true extent. Closer inspection of a moderately large sunspot shows a darker central region, the *umbra*, and a paler outer *penumbra* as shown in Figure 3.1.

Figure 3.1

The appearance of a typical sunspot

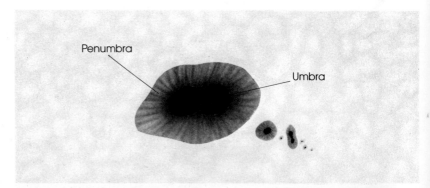

Sunspots are actually very bright objects which appear dark by contrast against the more brilliant solar disc. At a temperature approximately 2000 degrees Celsius below the rest of the Sun's surface the umbra appears darkest, with the penumbra less dark. Complex sunspots have several umbral and penumbral regions.

Depending on size, a sunspot can last from a few hours for small 'pores' to several months for large groups. They represent regions where the Sun's magnetic field is more concentrated, and survive while the intense field persists. Other types of activity may take place near sunspots, such as *solar flares*, bright filaments erupting from the Sun. Charged particles released during a flare travel across space to reach the Earth in about two days, disrupting radio communications. Light from the flare, travelling at nearly 300 000 kilometres per second, arrives after a delay of 8.3 minutes.

Flares last for a few minutes and are rarely bright enough to be noticed, but large *prominences* are generally longer lived and may be seen projecting from the eclipsed Sun. Some 'arch' prominences reach heights of over 300 000 kilometres and stretch over 1 000 000 kilometres (Figure 3.2 and Plate 4). Magnetism plays a part in shaping these features which, like flares, often erupt and disperse above active sunspots.

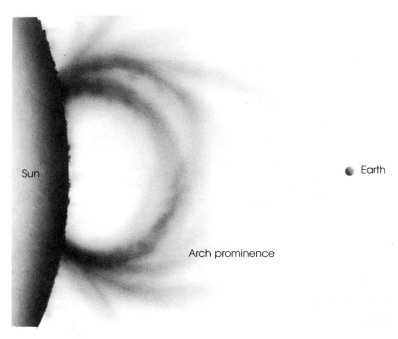

Figure 3.2

A large arch prominence, with the Earth drawn to scale for comparison

Sun

Earth

Arch prominence

GRANULATION

If the atmosphere is steady, high resolution views of the Sun reveal a mottled appearance to its surface. This is due to *convection* in the outer regions of the Sun, where columns of hotter gas rise to the surface, cool, then descend. Bright granules represent rising convection cells about 1500 kilometres in diameter, with the darker regions signalling downflow.

Figure 3.3

Granulation on the
Sun, caused by
convection currents

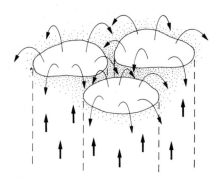

Larger bright patches, known as *faculae*, may be seen on
occasions near the Sun's limb (edge), features which usually
herald the appearance, or mark the disappearance, of a
sunspot group.

SOLAR ROTATION

Throughout the course of a year, the Sun presents a slowly
changing aspect as shown in Figure 3.4. Following the motion
of sunspots across the Sun's disc reveals that the Sun is
rotating, but not as a solid body. A sunspot near the Sun's
equator, for example, will cross the visible disc, disappear
behind the Sun's limb and return to its original position after
25.4 days, while nearer the poles this becomes closer to 34
days. Sunspots will evolve during this period and may show
motions of their own, making this type of observation
particularly fascinating.

January   May   September

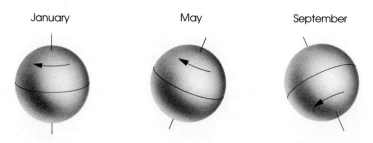

Figure 3.4

The changing
orientation of the Sun

THE SOLAR CYCLE

Observing the Sun regularly over several years, an astronomer
would notice a gradual change in the level of activity on its
surface. Starting from a time when virtually no sunspots can
be seen, the onset of activity is marked by the appearance of a
few small spots placed well away from the Sun's equator. For
a year or two there may be times when the 'quiet' Sun is

Figure 3.5

Sunspot distribution
in the quiet and active
Sun

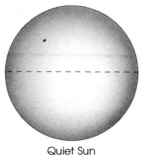

Quiet Sun

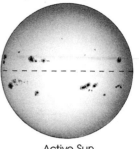

Active Sun

featureless, with only an occasional large spot to reward patient observation. As more sunspots begin to appear, their positions become closer to the Sun's equator (see Figure 3.5) until, after about five years, a large number may be seen at the same time in two 'belts'.

Over the next six years or so the number of sunspots declines, then the cycle repeats itself. The overall sequence of events takes just over 11 years, but can vary in length and successive maxima also vary in intensity. The solar cycle was first noticed (by an amateur astronomer) during observations made between 1826 and 1851.

Records indicate that the pattern has recurred continuously, except for the period 1645 to 1715 (the *Maunder minimum*), when the Sun endured a prolonged quiet phase, the cause of which is unknown. There may have been earlier quiet periods, but the records are incomplete.

Butterfly diagrams

A record of solar activity plotted as shown in Figure 3.6, with the position of each sunspot plotted on the *y*-axis and time on the *x*-axis, has become known as a *butterfly diagram*. The reason for this is that the variation in number and position of sunspots during the cycle gives the plot an appearance similar to a butterfly's wings.

Figure 3.6

A butterfly diagram for
the Sun

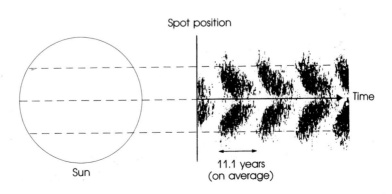

Spot position

Time

Sun

11.1 years
(on average)

ECLIPSES OF THE SUN

The Moon can pass between the Earth and the Sun. When all three bodies line up perfectly, an *eclipse* will be visible from parts of the Earth's surface which lie in the Moon's shadow. Depending on your position in the shadow, the eclipse may be total (Figure 3.7(a)) or partial (Figure 3.7(b)). A total eclipse of the Sun is a magnificent sight. The next one visible from Britain will take place in August 1999. For more information see p. 125.

Figure 3.7

A total eclipse of the Sun (a) only occurs when the Moon passes directly in front of the Sun as seen from Earth – otherwise the eclipse is partial (b)

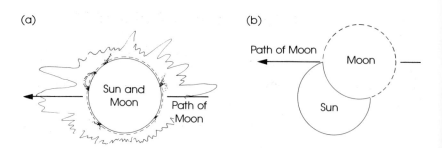

SOLAR POWER

At the Sun's core is a power supply releasing vast amounts of energy each second as a result of a type of nuclear reaction called *fusion*. Under the extreme conditions at the centre of the Sun, atoms are broken up, so normal chemical burning can not be taking place – the Sun is too hot to burn! Fusion in the Sun uses up pieces of hydrogen atoms and produces pieces of helium atoms:

$$\text{Hydrogen} \xrightarrow{\text{nuclear fusion}} \text{Helium} + \text{Energy}$$

This type of process requires the exceptionally high temperatures found at the Sun's core. The energy released works its way to the surface, slowly, and is radiated into space. This is the basic difference between a star and a planet: a star produces its own light, while a planet shines by reflecting the light of a nearby star.

If nuclear fusion could be achieved in a controlled way on Earth, it would provide an efficient, clean and almost endless energy supply. The process taking place in our present nuclear reactors, *fission*, has the disadvantage of producing generally higher levels of radioactivity. The development of fusion reactors would definitely bring a little sunshine to the energy crisis.

THE SUN'S FUTURE

In around five thousand million years the Sun will have exhausted its available core hydrogen and will swell into an enormous *red giant*, ending life on Earth. By then, we will have found a means of escape, or will have no need of one. After ejecting its outer layers into space, the Sun will die quietly as a *white dwarf* star, cooling and fading over countless years (see Chapter 5).

SUGGESTIONS FOR PROJECTS

1 Using projection, follow the progress of a sunspot across the Sun. Time how long it takes for the sunspot to cross a given fraction of the Sun's disc, and so calculate the time taken for the Sun to rotate.

2 Sketch the changing appearance of a sunspot or spot group as it evolves.

3 Construct a sundial which uses the shadow of a stick to tell the time.

QUESTIONS

1 What is the difference between a star and a planet?

2 A sunspot shines more brightly than an arc lamp. Why does it appear dark on the Sun?

3 A sunspot is first seen at the centre of the Sun somewhere along the line X–Y in the diagram below.

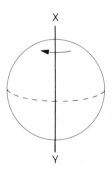

The sunspot takes 6.8 days to just disappear round the edge of the disc. What time does this observation give for the rotation period of the Sun? Copy the diagram and draw in likely initial position(s) of the spot.

31

WORDFINDER ON THE SUN

Copy the grid below (or photocopy this page – teachers, please see note at the front of the book). Use the clues to find the ten words or phrases hidden in the grid. The words can read horizontally, vertically and diagonally. Do not write on this page.

1 Source of the Sun's energy (6)
2 Dark region on the Sun (7)
3 Safe way to observe the Sun (10)
4 Material thrown off the Sun (10)
5 The edge of the Sun's disc (4)

6 The Sun is one of these (4)
7 Mottling on the Sun (11)
8 The commonest element in the Sun (8)
9 Long period of solar inactivity (7, 7)
10 Can pass in front of the Sun (4)

B	C	A	P	R	O	J	E	C	T	I	O	N	O	M
S	U	L	O	R	F	P	A	N	I	L	S	E	A	B
A	R	T	O	L	E	R	S	I	P	O	D	I	W	Y
P	R	O	M	I	N	E	N	C	E	N	S	T	A	R
L	B	O	F	G	R	T	Y	E	G	A	W	O	L	Y
O	S	B	E	L	F	E	O	S	R	E	P	D	I	B
T	A	U	L	O	R	N	D	K	A	L	C	L	O	R
M	A	U	N	D	E	R	M	I	N	I	M	U	M	E
R	O	F	E	S	S	L	A	J	U	K	O	R	N	D
A	L	E	U	N	P	R	L	R	L	M	O	W	A	F
M	Y	I	P	S	T	O	B	T	A	A	N	R	P	U
L	O	N	M	P	O	F	T	A	T	M	O	E	N	S
S	I	R	A	B	N	E	V	M	I	E	L	F	P	I
H	T	A	O	W	X	I	D	L	O	A	K	D	A	O
V	O	H	Y	D	R	O	G	E	N	R	E	L	P	N

THE SOLAR SPECTRUM

When we look at the Sun we see the bright surface or *photosphere*, upon which there may or may not be sunspots. But by visual observation alone we could not learn a great deal about the Sun; most of our knowledge has been obtained by instruments based upon the principle of the *spectroscope*.

A spectroscope splits light up and tells us which materials exist in the light-source. The first attempt at studying the spectrum of the Sun was made by Isaac Newton in 1666. He passed a beam of sunlight through a glass prism (Figure 3.8) and found that the light was spread out into a rainbow, from red at one end through orange, yellow, green and blue, to indigo and violet at the other end. We now know that light is a wave motion, with red light having the longest wavelength and violet the shortest (Figure 3.9). The prism bends or *refracts* the different wavelengths by different amounts – the shorter the wavelength, the greater the refraction. This is why the rainbow is produced. This is termed a *continuous spectrum*.

Figure 3.8

The production of a continuous spectrum from white light using a prism

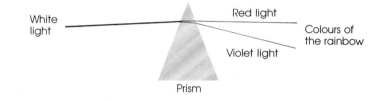

Figure 3.9

Red light has a longer wavelength than blue or violet

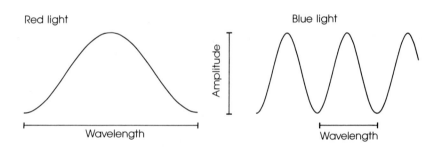

A continuous spectrum is produced by an *incandescent* solid, liquid, or gas at high pressure. If, however, we examine the spectrum of a gas at lower pressure, we will see no rainbow; instead there will be disconnected bright lines, each of which is due to one definite element or group of elements. This is termed an *emission* spectrum. The pattern of lines cannot be duplicated; thus if we see two bright yellow lines in a particular position, we know that they can only be due to one particular element, sodium.

The Sun's photosphere produces a continuous or rainbow spectrum. Above it are more rarefied gases. On their own, they would produce a bright-line emission spectrum, but as light is absorbed against the rainbow background they are reversed, and appear dark. The result is an *absorption* spectrum (Figure 3.10).

Figure 3.10

An absorption spectrum consists of dark lines against a continuous (rainbow) background

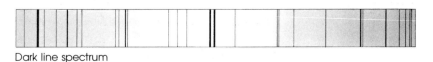

Dark line spectrum

33

The positions and intensities of the lines are not affected. For example, we can see two dark lines in the yellow part of the solar spectrum; these must be due to sodium – and we can prove that there is sodium in the Sun. At the present time over 70 elements have been identified. Hydrogen is by far the most abundant; next in order comes the second lightest element, helium.

STRUCTURE OF THE SUN

By now we have at least a fairly good idea of the way in which the Sun is made up. There is a central core, with about 25% of the total radius, where the temperature is of the order of 15 000 000 degrees Celsius; this is the Sun's 'powerhouse', where the energy is being produced. Beyond the core, extending out to 70% of the radius, is the *radiative zone*, where energy is transferred only by radiative processes; surrounding this is the turbulent *convective zone*, where the gases are rising and falling. The convective zone extends out to the photosphere, which has a relatively sharp boundary (Figure 3.11).

Hydrogen, which makes up about 70% of the Sun, is the solar 'fuel'. In the core, where the temperatures and pressures are tremendous, the hydrogen is being converted into helium. It takes four hydrogen nuclei to make one nucleus of helium; every time this happens, a little energy is set free and a little mass is lost. It is this energy which keeps the Sun shining, while the loss in mass amounts to 4 000 000 tonnes per second. This sounds a great deal – the Sun 'weighs' much less now than it did when you started reading this page – but the Sun is so large and massive that it will not change much for several thousands of millions of years yet.

Figure 3.11

The structure of the Sun

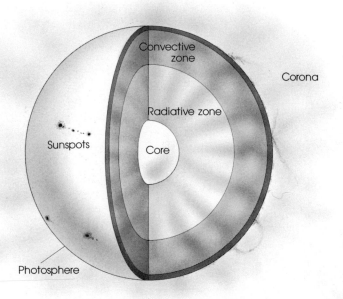

Convective zone

Corona

Radiative zone

Sunspots

Core

Photosphere

RADIATION AND SOLAR WIND

The Sun is emitting particles and radiation constantly; what we cannot see we are able to detect with special equipment.

Among these particles are neutrinos which have no mass and no electrical charge. They are very difficult to detect, but they can be trapped by some liquids, so that a 'neutrino telescope' is actually a large tank. To shield the detectors from other particles which would produce similar effects, they have to be set deep inside the Earth. At Homestake Mine, in South Dakota, a neutrino detector has been installed a mile below ground in a working goldmine.

At the moment it seems that the Sun is sending out far fewer neutrinos than in theory it ought to do, and the reasons for this remain unknown. The 'neutrino problem' is in fact one of the most difficult questions facing solar physicists at the present time.

Active regions on the Sun send out streams of atomic particles in all directions, making up what is called the *solar wind*. (It is particles from the solar wind which overload the Earth's Van Allen belts and cascade down into the upper atmosphere, producing aurorae.) The solar wind extends far beyond all the planets in the Solar System, and has no definite boundary. The region where it ceases to be detectable is called the *heliopause*, and the region where it can be measured is the *heliosphere*.

SOLAR ECLIPSES

When the New Moon passes between the Sun and the Earth, it hides the Sun and produces a solar eclipse. If the lining-up is exact we see a total eclipse, which never lasts for more than $7\frac{1}{2}$ minutes and generally much less; if the alignment is not perfect, the eclipse is partial (Figure 3.12). If exact alignment occurs when the Moon is near apogee, the Moon's disc is not large enough to cover the Sun completely, and a ring of sunlight is left showing around the dark body of the Moon. This is termed an annular eclipse, from the Latin *annulus*, a ring (see Figure 3.13, on the next page).

(a)

(b)
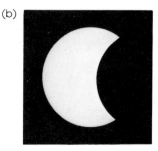

Figure 3.12

(a) A total eclipse of the Sun and (b) a partial eclipse

Since the Moon's shadow is only just long enough to reach us, total eclipses are rare as seen from any particular point on the Earth. Thus the last total eclipse visible from any part of Britain was that of 1927, while the next will not be until 11 August

Figure 3.13

Some stages in the progress of an annular eclipse of the Sun

1999. A list of eclipses for the period from 1988 to 1999 is given in Appendix II.

A total eclipse is a magnificent sight. As soon as the Sun has been completely covered, we see the solar atmosphere or *chromosphere* in which there may be some prominences; these were formerly known as 'red flames', but the name is misleading, since a prominence is not a flame, but a mass of glowing hydrogen. Beyond the chromosphere comes the outer atmosphere or *corona*, which stretches out across the sky. As totality ends, a tiny part of the bright surface reappears from behind the Moon, producing the lovely 'diamond ring' effect, and at once the chromosphere, prominences and corona disappear. In mid-totality the sky may become dark enough for planets and bright stars to be seen.

THE SOLAR CORONA

The corona has no definite boundary, but simply thins out with increasing distance from the Sun. It is very rarefied – many millions of times less dense than the air we breathe – and its shape and form are affected by the state of the sunspot cycle. Because its atoms and molecules are moving around at tremendous speeds it has a high 'temperature', but it contains so little mass that there is not much 'heat'.

With the naked eye, the chromosphere, prominences and corona can be seen only during a total eclipse, but spectroscopic equipment makes it possible to study the chromosphere and prominences at any time.

THE SOLAR CYCLE

Many sunspots occur in pairs (or pairs of groups), with one showing north magnetic polarity, and the other south (Figure 3.14). The connection betwen sunspots and magnetism is established, but the cause of the solar cycle is not known. One idea concerns the 'wrapping up' of the Sun's magnetic field due to differential rotation, while a more recent theory ties in the movement of spots with the movement of giant convection cells from polar regions towards the equator (Figures 3.15 and 3.16).

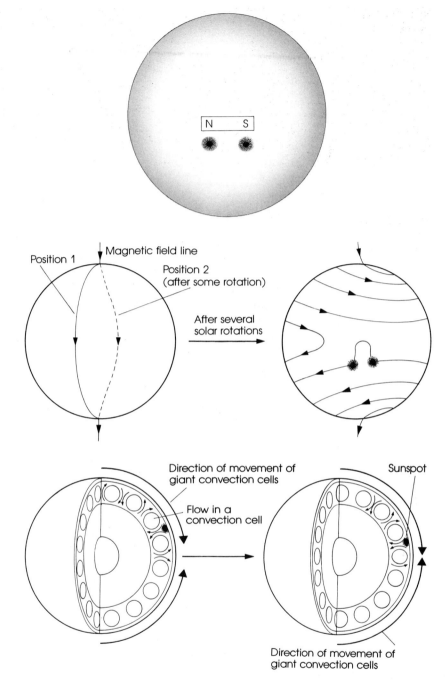

Figure 3.14

The magnetic field associated with a sunspot pair is similar to that of a bar magnet below the Sun's surface

Figure 3.15

According to one theory, the sunspot cycle's pattern results from the 'wrapping up' of magnetic field lines due to the unequal rotation of parts of the Sun's disc

Position 1

Magnetic field line

Position 2 (after some rotation)

After several solar rotations

Figure 3.16

An alternative idea suggests that downward flow in moving convection cells concentrates the Sun's magnetic field, so producing sunspots which follow the movement of the cells towards the Sun's equator

Direction of movement of giant convection cells

Flow in a convection cell

Sunspot

Direction of movement of giant convection cells

The inconstant Sun

We have seen that in some ways the Sun must be regarded as a variable star. The average length of the sunspot cycle is 11 years, but this is not constant, and magnetic phenomena (the reversal of paired sunspot polarities in each solar hemisphere) indicate that the true cycle is not 11 years, but 22. Whether the solar cycle has any effect upon the Earth's weather is by no means certain, but it may be significant that during the Maunder minimum of 1645–1715, when there were almost no sunspots, the weather in Europe was bitterly cold. Frost fairs were held during winter on the frozen River Thames.

It is also possible that slight changes in the Sun's output have been responsible for the ice ages which have affected the Earth throughout its history, the last of which ended a mere 10 000 years ago. In any case it is fortunate for us that the Sun is a relatively stable star. If it became slightly hotter or colder, all life on our world might well be wiped out.

SUGGESTIONS FOR PROJECTS

3 Draw some sunspot groups in detail. Watch for the *Wilson effect* (see diagram below).

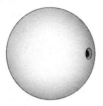  

The Wilson effect. The umbra of a sunspot appears to be closer to the inner edge of the penumbra when the sunspot is situated near the Sun's limb (edge)

4 Make daily records of the noon temperature and the rainfall, and see whether you can find any connection between your local weather and the numbers of sunspot groups.

5 If an eclipse is due, make sketches at regular intervals to show how the Moon first covers and then uncovers the Sun.

6 If you have access to a direct vision spectroscope, point it at a bright sky (*not* at the Sun). Note the dark absorption lines (Fraunhofer lines) in the continuous spectrum, and see if you can identify any line patterns mentioned in the text (e.g. sodium).

QUESTIONS

4 Explain how the dark lines in the Sun's spectrum are produced.

5 Why is the Sun losing mass – and how much mass is being lost every second?

6 During an annular eclipse of the Sun, can you see the corona and prominences with the naked eye? If not, why not?

7 The maximum duration of a total lunar eclipse (approximately 100 minutes) is greater than the maximum length of totality during a solar eclipse (approximately $7\frac{1}{2}$ minutes). Explain why this is so.

PLANETS, COMETS AND METEORS

The Solar System is made up of one star (the Sun), the nine planets, the planetary satellites, asteroids or minor planets, comets and meteoroids. Even Jupiter, much the largest and most massive of the planets, has less than one-thousandth the mass of the Sun. It is thought that the Solar System was produced by the build-up by *accretion* of material from a cloud or *solar nebula* associated with the youthful Sun. The Earth and the Moon are known to be about 4700 million years old, and the remaining planets are presumably of the same age. A summary of data for the planets is shown below.

Planet	Mean distance from Sun (millions of kilometres)	Orbital period	Rotation period	Diameter (kilometres)	Relative mass (Earth = 1)
Mercury	57.9	88 days	58.6 days	4 879	0.06
Venus	108.2	224.7 days	243.1 days	12 104	0.82
Earth	149.6	365.3 days	23 h 56 m	12 756	1
Mars	227.9	687.0 days	24 h 37 m	6 794	0.11
Jupiter	778.3	11.9 years	9 h 50 m	143 884	318
Saturn	1427.0	29.5 years	10 h 39 m	120 536	95
Uranus	2869.6	84.0 years	17 h 14 m	50 724	15
Neptune	4496.7	164.8 years	17 h 52 m	50 538	17
Pluto	5900	247.7 years	6.4 days	2 445	0.01

The planetary system is divided into two parts. First we have four relatively small, solid worlds. Then comes a wide gap, in which move thousands of small worlds known as asteroids, and then come the four giants, which have gaseous surfaces, with solid cores and globes made up largely of liquid. Pluto, which is now known to be smaller than the Moon, may not be worthy of true planetary status. The relative sizes of the planets are shown on the next page, in Figure 4.1.

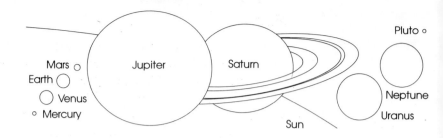

Figure 4.1

The Sun and planets drawn to scale (see also Plates 5–12)

THE PLANETS

Mercury

Mercury is not a great deal larger than the Moon, and its low escape velocity (4.3 kilometres per second) means that it can retain only a very rarefied atmosphere. Little detail on its surface can be seen from Earth, even with large telescopes, and almost all our knowledge comes from the pictures sent back by *Mariner 10* in 1973 and 1974, the only spacecraft to have passed by Mercury as yet. The surface is not unlike that of the Moon (Plate 5), with mountains and craters. The temperature during the long 'day' is very high; if you could put a tin kettle on to the rocks there, around noon, the kettle would melt! The existence of any life there can certainly be ruled out.

Venus

Venus is very different from Mercury. In size and mass it is almost a twin of the Earth, but it is in a very different state, presumably because it is considerably closer to the Sun. From Earth we can never see its true surface, because of its dense, cloudy atmosphere (Plate 6). Again we depend upon spacecraft, some of which have been put into orbit round the planet, mapping the surface by radar; while others have made controlled landings there and have sent back pictures.

Venus' thick atmosphere is made up chiefly of the heavy, unbreathable gas carbon dioxide, which blankets in the Sun's heat and makes the surface intolerably hot – almost 500 degrees Celsius. The atmospheric pressure is 90 times that of the Earth's air at sea level, and the clouds contain large amounts of sulphuric acid, so that although Venus has been named in honour of the Goddess of Beauty, the surface conditions are much more like the conventional idea of hell. There are mountains, craters and probably active volcanoes. The 'day' is very long – Venus has a rotation period longer than its orbital period, for reasons which remain unknown – and more curious still, the planet spins from east to west, the opposite way to Earth. Like Mercury, Venus has no satellite.

Mars

Mars, the next planet out from Earth, can never come as close to us as Venus, but is much easier to observe. It has a low escape velocity (5 kilometres per second) and a thin, carbon dioxide atmosphere which is much more rarefied than the Earth's air at the summit of Mount Everest. The Martian day or *sol* is about half an hour longer than ours, so that there are 669 sols in a Martian year. At the equator the days are reasonably warm, but nights anywhere on the planet are bitterly cold, partly because of the thinness of the atmosphere and partly because Mars is much further away from the Sun.

Telescopes show white polar caps, icy in nature, with red 'deserts' and darker areas. The deserts are coated with reddish minerals rather than sand, and the dark areas are not seas or old sea-beds, as used to be thought, but are merely regions where the reddish material has been removed by the Martian winds. The most prominent dark region is known as the Syrtis Major (see Figure 4.2).

Figure 4.2

A sketch of Mars, showing the prominent dark feature known as Syrtis Major

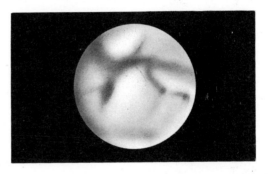

The first successful space probe to Mars, *Mariner 4* in 1965, showed that the surface is cratered, with mountains and valleys. Later space vehicles showed huge volcanoes, one of which, Olympus Mons (Mount Olympus) is three times as high as Mount Everest. There are also features which seem to be dry riverbeds, in which case Mars must once have had much more atmosphere than it has now.

Two spacecraft, *Viking 1* and *Viking 2*, made controlled landings on Mars in 1976, and sent back pictures showing a red, barren landscape under a pink sky (Plate 7). Both *Viking* probes 'scooped up' samples of the surface materials, analysed them, and transmitted the results back to Earth. No definite sign of life was found and it now seems likely that no living things inhabit Mars, though we cannot be certain of this until samples are brought back and studied in our laboratories.

Mars has two satellites, Phobos and Deimos, both of which are less than 30 kilometres in diameter and relatively close to Mars. They may be captured asteroids, and have been shown to be irregular, crater-scarred lumps of rock. Neither object would be of much use as a source of light during the Martian night.

Asteroids

Beyond Mars are found the asteroids or minor planets. Only one (Ceres) is as much as 900 kilometres in diameter (Figure 4.3), and only one (Vesta) is ever visible to the naked eye. It was once thought that they might be the remains of an old planet which broke up, but it is now generally believed that no large body could form in that region of the Solar System because of the powerful disruptive pull of Jupiter.

Figure 4.3

The size of Ceres compared with the British Isles and part of Europe

Ceres

Ceres, the largest of the asteroids, was also the first to be discovered, in 1801. A mathematical relationship known as Bode's law had predicted that a planet might exist in the region between the orbits of Mars and Jupiter, but all the asteroids combined would not form one body as massive as the Moon, and in any case it is not likely that Bode's law has any real significance.

The most interesting asteroids are those which move away from the main swarm. Some pass close to Earth (Hermes, in 1937, passed by at only twice the distance of the Moon), but all these are very small.

Jupiter

Far beyond the main asteroid group moves Jupiter, which is more massive than all the other planets put together. It is very brilliant, and becomes well placed for observation with a small telescope about a month later each year. Its 'year' is almost 12 times as long as ours, but it spins quickly on its axis, and at the equator the rotation period is only 9 hours and 50 minutes. However, Jupiter has a gaseous surface, and different parts of it rotate at different speeds. Near the poles the rotation period is several minutes longer than that at the equator. Because it spins so rapidly, the globe is appreciably flattened, as any small telescope will show (Figure 4.4).

Figure 4.4

A telescopic view of
Jupiter

Telescopes reveal that the planet has a yellow surface, crossed by dark streaks known as belts. These belts are regions where gas is descending, while the bright zones occur where the gas is rising. The surface details are always changing. Generally there are two conspicuous belts, one to either side of the equator, and there are spots, wisps and festoons (Plate 8). Particularly notable is the Great Red Spot, which is oval, and is now known to be a whirling storm, probably owing its colour to phosphorus.

According to the latest models, Jupiter has a rocky core at a temperature of about 30 000 degrees Celsius, surrounded by layers of liquid hydrogen – metallic in its lower parts, molecular in the higher regions. Above the liquid comes the gaseous 'atmosphere', made up chiefly of hydrogen (89%) and helium (11%).

Four space probes have passed by Jupiter: two *Pioneers* (1973 and 1974) and two *Voyagers* (1979). Most of our detailed knowledge of the planet has been drawn from these missions. It has been found that there is a very powerful magnetic field, together with zones of radiation strong enough to kill any astronaut foolish enough to enter them. There is a thin, dark ring system, invisible from Earth and quite unlike the glorious ring system of Saturn.

Jupiter has a whole family of satellites. Four of them – Io, Europa, Ganymede and Callisto – have been known since 1610 and can be seen with any small telescope. They are of planetary size (see Figure 4.5, on the next page) and only Europa is smaller than our Moon; Ganymede is actually larger than Mercury, though not so massive. All have low escape velocities, and have no appreciable atmosphere. Data for the four large satellites are shown on the next page.

Figure 4.5

Jupiter's 'Galilean'
satellites compared to
the Earth's satellite
(the Moon)

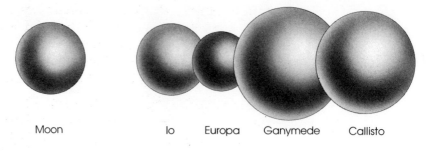

Moon   Io   Europa   Ganymede   Callisto

Satellite	*Mean distance from Jupiter* (kilometres)	*Revolution period* (days)	*Diameter* (kilometres)
Io	421 600	1.8	3642
Europa	670 900	3.6	3130
Ganymede	1 070 000	7.2	5268
Callisto	1 880 000	16.7	4806

It is fascinating to follow these satellites from night to night. They pass in transit across Jupiter's disc, and their shadows can also be seen in transit; they may be *occulted* (i.e., hidden) by Jupiter, or eclipsed by its shadow.

The *Voyager* pictures showed that Ganymede and Callisto are icy and cratered, while Europa has an icy surface which is as smooth as a snooker ball. Io is different – it is sulphur-covered, with violently active sulphur volcanoes (see cover illustration). Io also has a marked effect upon the strong radio emissions sent out by Jupiter itself.

Saturn

Saturn (Plate 9), second of the giant planets, is smaller than Jupiter, but still much larger than Earth. It too has a rocky core surrounded by liquid hydrogen, with a gaseous surface, but it is less dense and less massive than Jupiter, and the

Figure 4.6

Saturn's flattened
globe and rings

mean density of its globe is actually less than that of water. There are belts, though not so prominent as those of Jupiter, with occasional spots, and there are no features as striking as Jupiter's Great Red Spot. Like Jupiter, Saturn rotates rapidly on its axis, and its globe is obviously flattened (Figure 4.6).

Saturn's rings are superb (Plate 10). They are not solid or liquid, and in fact no such ring could exist, as it would at once be broken up by Saturn's strong pull of gravity. They are made up of millions of small icy particles, all speeding round Saturn like dwarf moonlets. There are two main rings, A and B, separated by a gap which is known as Cassini's division in honour of its discoverer (Figure 4.7) and there is a semi-transparent ring, C, closer to the planet. All these can be seen with a small telescope when well placed. The *Voyager* spacecraft of 1980 and 1981 showed that the rings are much more complicated than had been expected, with thousands of ringlets and narrow divisions; even the Cassini division is not empty. *Voyager* also detected several new rings which cannot be seen from Earth.

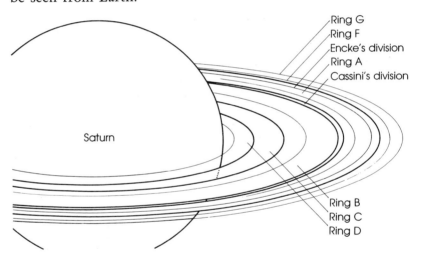

Figure 4.7

Saturn's ring system

Ring G
Ring F
Encke's division
Ring A
Cassini's division

Saturn

Ring B
Ring C
Ring D

The rings are very extensive, but are also very thin – probably less than a kilometre thick – so that when they are placed edgewise-on to the Earth they almost disappear (see Figure 4.8, on the next page). The best views are obtained when the rings are tilted towards us, as was the case during the late 1980s.

The origin of the rings is uncertain. They may have been produced by the break-up of an old satellite, but it is more likely that they were formed from material which never collected into a larger body.

Saturn, like Jupiter, has a family of satellites. Those with diameters of 200 kilometres or more are detailed on the next page.

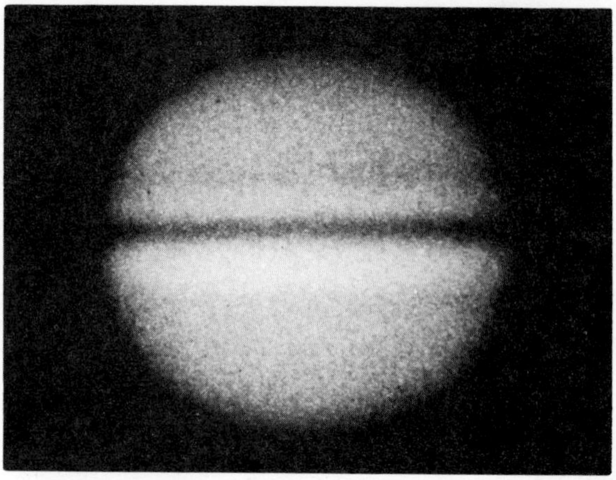

Figure 4.8

Saturn photographed
with its rings edge-on,
as viewed from Earth

Satellite	Mean distance from Saturn (kilometres)	Revolution period (days)	Maximum diameter (kilometres)
Mimas	151 420	0.9	398
Enceladus	185 540	1.4	498
Tethys	238 040	1.9	1046
Dione	294 670	2.7	1120
Rhea	377 420	4.5	1528
Titan	527 040	15.9	5150
Hyperion	1 221 860	21.3	360
Iapetus	3 561 000	79.3	1436
Phoebe	12 954 000	550.4	220

Voyager results showed that most of the satellites are icy and cratered, but Enceladus is fairly smooth, while Iapetus is unusual in having one hemisphere which is as bright as ice and the other which is as dark as a blackboard. The reason for this is unknown, though it seems that part of the satellite is covered by blackish material which has welled up from inside the globe.

Much the most interesting satellite is Titan, which has a dense atmosphere made up largely of nitrogen. The *Voyager* pictures showed merely the upper cloud layer, and we still do not know much about the nature of the surface. There may be oceans of liquid methane, cliffs of solid methane, and a methane rain dripping down from the orange clouds in the nitrogen sky.

Uranus

Uranus, the next giant planet, is so remote that no Earth-based telescope will show much detail on its pale greenish disc. It is notable because of its strange axial tilt. The axis is inclined to the orbit at more than a right angle (Figure 4.9) so that at times, as during the 1980s, one pole is

Figure 4.9

The unusual tilt of
Uranus

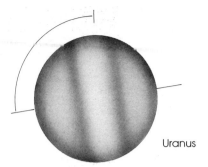

Uranus

turned towards the Sun and the Earth. During Uranus' 'year', which is 84 times as long as ours, each pole has a 'midnight sun' lasting for 21 Earth-years and a 'night' of equal length. In 1977 it was found that there is a system of dark, narrow rings, very difficult to detect from Earth.

One probe has passed by Uranus. This was *Voyager 2*, which did so in January 1986. It was found that there is a magnetic field, but the magnetic axis is inclined to the rotational axis by 60 degrees – a case unique in the Solar System. *Voyager 2* also surveyed the satellites, of which 15 are now known, although only five (Miranda, Ariel, Umbriel, Titania and Oberon) are large enough to be seen from Earth. None has a diameter as great as that of the Moon. Miranda has a remarkably varied surface, with craters, peaks, ice-cliffs, and appears to have been broken up and reformed several times! (Plate 11)

Neptune

Neptune, last of the giants, was tracked down in 1846 because of the irregularities it had been causing in the movements of Uranus. It is slightly smaller than Uranus, but rather more massive. The two are alike in many ways – they seem to have solid cores and gaseous surfaces, but contain much more water and ammonia than Jupiter or Saturn.

Neptune has at least three satellites. One (Triton) is large, and may have an atmosphere, while another (Nereid) is very small, with a very elliptical orbit. *Voyager 2* passed by Neptune in August 1989.

Pluto

Finally there is Pluto, discovered by Clyde Tombaugh in 1930. It has a strange eccentric orbit, which periodically brings it closer in than Neptune, though the orbital inclination of 17 degrees means that there is no danger of a collision between the two. Pluto is smaller than the Moon, and is probably made up of a mixture of rock and ice. Its atmosphere is very thin and the surface temperature is very low. It is accompanied by a second body, Charon, which has about half the diameter of Pluto itself. Charon's revolution period is 6.4 days, and this is also the length of Pluto's axial rotation, so that to an observer on Pluto, Charon would appear fixed in the sky.

The whole nature of the Pluto–Charon pair remains uncertain. The two bodies do not seem to fit into the general pattern of the Solar System, and they may best be regarded as asteroidal. Moreover, there is every chance that another planet exists at a still greater distance from the Sun, but it is bound to be very faint, and will be hard to track down.

COMETS

Comets are the most erratic members of the Solar System. They move round the Sun, but most of them do so in highly elliptical orbits, so that we can see them only when they are travelling in the inner part of the system.

The only substantial part of a comet is the nucleus, which is icy in nature. Surrounding the nucleus is the head, made up of very thin gas and 'dust'. A large comet may have one or more tails, composed either of gas or dust (Plate 12), but many fainter comets never develop tails, and look simply like tiny patches of light in the sky.

Cometary tails always point more or less away from the Sun, so that when a comet is moving outwards it actually travels tail-first. Particles of a gas-tail are 'pushed out' by the pressure of sunlight (light can be thought of as particles called *photons* which are capable of exerting pressure), while the dust in a dust-tail is repelled by the solar wind. Generally a gas-tail is straight, while a dust-tail is curved (see Figure 4.10).

It is thought that comets are very ancient, and date back to the early history of the Solar System. According to one popular theory, there is a whole 'cloud' of comets moving round the Sun at an immense distance. This is known as the

Figure 4.10

The structure of a comet may include the head, dust-tail and gas-tail

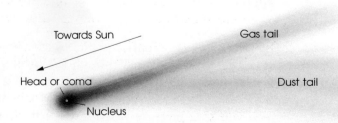

Towards Sun   Gas tail

Head or coma   Dust tail

Nucleus

Oort Cloud, after the Dutch astronomer who first suggested its existence. If a comet is disturbed for any reason, it begins to fall in towards the Sun, and eventually comes within our range. If it is not 'captured' by the gravitational pull of a planet, usually Jupiter, it will return to the Cloud after passing round the Sun and will not be seen again for thousands or even millions of years, which is why brilliant comets cannot be predicted and are always apt to take us by surprise. If, however, it is 'captured' it will be forced into a short-period orbit, and will return on a more regular basis. Encke's Comet does so every 3.3 years, so that we always know when and where to expect it.

Halley's Comet

Dozens of short-period comets are known, but most of them are faint, because they lose material every time they pass close to the Sun and lose some of their ices by evaporation. The only periodical comet which can ever become brilliant is Halley's, which has a period of 76 years. It last returned in 1986, but was poorly placed, and never became as conspicuous as it had been at the two most recent earlier returns, those of 1835 and 1910. Five spacecraft were sent to it, and one of these, the European vehicle *Giotto*, passed through the head, sending back close-range pictures of the nucleus, which proved to be covered with a blackish deposit. Halley's Comet will next return in the year 2061.

Remember that a comet lies far beyond the Earth's atmosphere, so that it does not seem to move quickly against the starry background. You have to watch it for hours to notice that it is shifting at all.

METEOR SHOWERS

One periodical comet, Biela's, used to have a period of 6.7 years, and was seen regularly. At its return in 1846 it surprised astronomers by breaking in two. It was last seen at the return of 1852, and has certainly disintegrated, but for some years meteors were seen coming from the position where the comet ought to have been. This was convincing proof of a close association between comets and meteors (or shooting stars as they are commonly known).

Meteors tend to travel round the Sun in shoals. Each time we pass through a shoal, we see a shower of shooting stars. Because the meteors in a shoal are moving in parallel paths, they seem to issue from one set point in the sky, known as the *radiant* (Figure 4.11). There are many annual showers, of

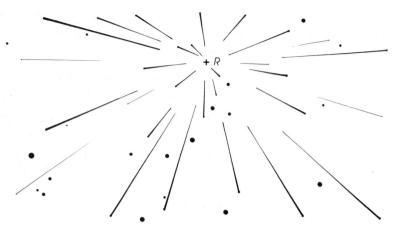

Figure 4.11

Shower meteors appear to come from a point on the sky (the radiant – *R*)

which the most brilliant is the Perseid shower of August, so named because its radiant lies in the constellation of Perseus.

There are also *sporadic* meteors, which are not members of a particular shower, and may appear from any direction at any moment.

The Solar System is a fascinating place. Though it may be insignificant in the universe as a whole, it is of vital importance to us; after all, it is our home.

SUGGESTIONS FOR PROJECTS

1 Make a cardboard model of the Solar System, showing the orbits of (a) the planets out as far as Mars and (b) the outer planets, with the orbit of Mars as a comparison.

2 Make a model to show the Earth's orbit compared to that of a typical comet.

3 Check up in an astronomical almanac, and identify any planets which are in view. Note their positions against the stars from night to night, and see how they are moving. (For the slower-moving planets this will mean observing over a period of weeks.)

4 Make a model of Saturn's ring system, and use it to explain the changing angle from which we view the rings.

5 Use diagrams or models to show the behaviour of a comet's tail as the comet passes through perihelion.

(For telescope users)

6 Observe the changing phases of Venus, and note when it is at exact dichotomy (50% phase).

7 Observe the satellites of Jupiter from night to night, noting the various phenomena that they show (transit, shadow transit, eclipse, occultation).

8 Draw Saturn's rings, noting the Cassini division and also the shadows of the rings on the globe and the globe on the rings.

9 Identify Uranus, by using binoculars and a star chart. (The positions are given in yearly almanacs.)

10 During a meteor shower, see how many naked-eye meteors you can count over a period of half an hour. Then check to see whether they come from the shower radiant, or whether they are sporadic meteors.

QUESTIONS

1 Why can we see some surface detail on Mercury and Mars but not Venus?

2 What clues are there to the existence of liquid water at some time in Martian history?

3 In which part of the Solar System do most of the asteroids move?

4 Why do Saturn's rings sometimes disappear, as seen from Earth?

5 What is unusual about the spin of
(a) Venus?
(b) Uranus?

6 Pluto is widely regarded as being unworthy of true planetary status. Give reasons for this opinion.

7 Explain why
(a) most short period comets are faint
(b) cometary tails point away from the Sun.

THE MOVEMENTS OF THE PLANETS

The stars are so far away that they seem to keep the same patterns for year after year, century after century. The planets are so much closer that they seem to wander slowly around the sky, but their orbits are not sharply inclined to that of the Earth, so that they keep to a well-defined belt round the sky called the Zodiac. (Pluto, with an orbital inclination of 17 degrees, is the only exception.) Mercury, Venus, Mars, Jupiter and Saturn have been known since very ancient times. Of the rest, Uranus was discovered in 1781, Neptune in 1846 and Pluto as recently as 1930. Uranus can just be seen with the naked eye, but Neptune is too faint to be glimpsed without binoculars, and to see Pluto a telescope of reasonable size is needed.

INFERIOR PLANETS

Mercury and Venus are known as the inferior planets, because they are closer to the Sun than we are (Figure 4.12). They show phases like those of the Moon, and for much the same reason, though of course they travel round the Sun and not round the Earth. In position 1 in Figure 4.12, the planet is almost between us and the Sun, so that its dark side is turned towards us; it is 'new', and cannot be seen – unless it passes directly in front of the Sun, in transit, when it may be seen as a black disc against the solar face. This does not happen often. The last transit of Venus was that of 1882; the next will not be until 2004.

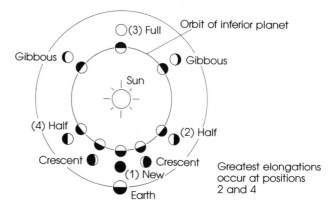

Figure 4.12

Positions of the inferior planets and the corresponding phases (seen from Earth)

As the planet moves in its orbit, it shows up as a crescent in the morning sky. At position 2 it appears as a half-phase (*dichotomy*); it then becomes gibbous, and in position 3 it is full, though it is then on the far side of the Sun and will be out of view. It then reappears as a gibbous object in the evening sky, becoming a half again in position 4 and then shrinking to a crescent before returning to new. When new it is said to be at *inferior conjunction*, when full, at *superior conjunction*; it is easiest to find at *elongation*.

Obviously, Mercury and Venus are best seen either in the west after sunset or in the east before dawn; they can never be seen all through the night. Mercury is never conspicuous, and is visible with the naked eye only when favourably placed. Venus can become bright enough to cast a shadow and when at its best, keen-sighted people can glimpse it without optical aid when the Sun is above the horizon.

SUPERIOR PLANETS

The superior planets – i.e., those further from the Sun than the Earth – appear to behave differently from Mercury and Venus, when seen from Earth. The orbit of Mars is shown in Figure 4.13, but the same principles apply to the other superior planets.

Mars is best seen when it is lined up with the Sun and the Earth (position M_1). It is then opposite the Sun in the sky, and is said to be at *opposition*. A year later, the Earth has completed one journey round the Sun, and has returned to position E_1; but Mars, moving more slowly in a larger orbit, has not had time to

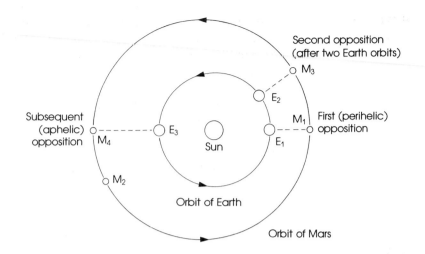

Figure 4.13

The motion of a
superior planet relative
to Earth, illustrated
using Mars

Second opposition
(after two Earth orbits)

M₃

Subsequent
(aphelic)
opposition

M₄

E₃

Sun

E₁

M₁   First (perihelic)
opposition

E₂

M₂

Orbit of Earth

Orbit of Mars

do so, and has only reached position M_2 after passing through
conjunction. The Earth has to 'catch Mars up', so to speak, and
does so only when it has reached position E_2, with Mars at M_3.
Oppositions of Mars occur only at mean intervals of 780 days;
the interval between one opposition and the next is known as
the *synodic period*. The other planets orbit more slowly, so that
their synodic periods are shorter.

Before and after opposition a superior planet will appear to
move 'backwards' against the stars for a while – east to west,
instead of west to east – because it is being 'passed' by the Earth
(Figure 4.14). This is known as moving in a *retrograde* sense. This
was well known to the ancient astronomers, and was early proof
that the planets do not revolve round the Earth in perfect
circles.

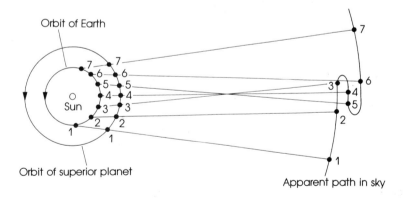

Figure 4.14

As the Earth 'overtakes'
Mars, the red planet
appears to change its
direction of movement
across the sky

Orbit of Earth

Sun

Orbit of superior planet

Apparent path in sky

However, most of the planets move round the Sun in paths
which are only slightly elliptical. Mars is something of an
exception; its distance from the Sun ranges between 206 700 000
kilometres at its nearest (*perihelion*) out to 249 100 000
kilometres at its furthest (*aphelion*). It is closest to the Earth
when perihelion and opposition occur at the same time (Figure
4.13, positions E_1 and M_1); thus in September 1988 the
minimum distance from Earth was only 58 400 000 kilometres

(Figure 4.13). It can never be seen as a half or a crescent, but when well away from opposition it may appear markedly gibbous.

It is not hard to identify the planets. Because the planets appear as tiny discs, rather than point sources of light, they twinkle less than stars.

KEPLER'S LAWS

The planet Mars, as we have seen, has a rather eccentric orbit. Early observations by Tycho Brahe (1546–1601) held clues to the elliptical orbit, and these were used by the great German astronomer Johannes Kepler together with other data to formulate three laws of planetary motion, between 1609 and 1618:

Kepler's first law A planet moves round the Sun in an elliptical orbit with the Sun at one focus.

Kepler's second law A line between the Sun and the planet sweeps out equal areas in equal times as the planet moves in its orbit.

Kepler's third law The square of the time taken to complete one orbit is proportional to the cube of the mean distance between the Sun and the planet. If the orbital period is measured in years (P) and the Sun–planet distance is in astronomical units (D) then Kepler's third law can be written

$$P^2 = D^3$$

The first and second laws are illustrated in Figure 4.15. Kepler used a blend of science and religious mysticism in his work. By combining the ideas of Copernicus, the observations of Tycho, and (incorrectly) assuming magnetism to be the driving force of planetary motion, he left an important legacy in his three laws. They can be used in accurately estimating the motion of any smaller body – a space probe, for example – under the gravitational influence of a larger one.

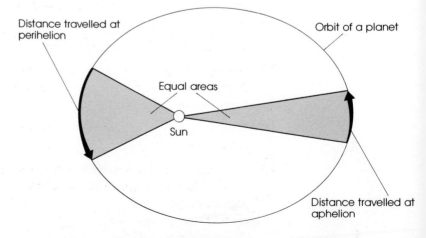

Figure 4.15

Illustration of Kepler's first and second laws

COMETARY ORBITS

As a comet swings inwards towards the Sun, its orbit may be changed if it passes close to a large planet. This is how the short period comets came into being. If the orbit is perturbed so as to turn it into an open curve (a *parabola* or *hyperbola*) then the comet will not return. So far, no comet has been observed with an orbit which suggests beyond doubt that it came from outside the Solar System. Their probable origin, the Oort Cloud, is thought to lie at a distance of around 60 000 astronomical units from the Sun.

UNIVERSAL GRAVITATION

Magnetism is not the driving force for planetary motion; we now know that the force of gravity regulates the Solar System. Isaac Newton developed a law of gravitation which tells us that the force F between two objects of mass M and m, separated by a distance d, is (G = Newton's gravitational constant):

$$F = \frac{GMm}{d^2}$$

This is an example of an inverse square law and shows that the force of attraction between two masses decreases relatively quickly as the distance between them increases. Newton recognised the value of Kepler's earlier work, and that of other scientists, even though it was wrong in places. He said: 'If I have seen further (than others) it is by standing on the shoulders of giants'.

QUESTIONS

8 Why do the bright planets always seem to stay within the Zodiac?

9 Why are Mercury and Venus difficult to see at full phase?

10 Jupiter comes to opposition only about a month later each year, but with Mars the interval between successive oppositions is over two years. Explain why this is so.

11 Explain the meaning of 'perihelion' and 'aphelion'. Why is Mars best seen at a perihelic opposition?

12 How is it generally believed that the planets were formed – and what is their approximate age?

13 When Mercury is in transit across the Sun as seen from the Earth, what would be the phase of the Earth as seen from the surface of Mercury?

14 Can the superior planets ever pass through (a) inferior conjunction, (b) superior conjunction?

15 An asteroid is discovered which has an orbital period of 8 years. What is its mean distance from the Sun, measured in astronomical units?

5

THE STARS

THE CONSTELLATIONS

Looking up to the sky on a clear, dark night, you might think you can see millions of stars. From a site away from street lights, the number will be nearer 2500. Even so, it may be difficult to pick out any patterns apart from the well-known examples such as the 'Big Dipper' or 'Plough' (Ursa Major, the Great Bear) and Orion in winter.

These *constellations* are made up of groups of stars which are not necessarily closely associated in space but which appear as patterns or groupings when viewed from Earth (see Figure 5.1). Numerous astronomers have imagined hundreds of groupings down the ages, but only 88 named constellations have survived. These are mostly connected with mythology, and very few resemble their name.

Figure 5.1

Bright stars in the constellation Cassiopeia – the reclining queen. Stars at different distances give rise to the characteristic 'W' shape

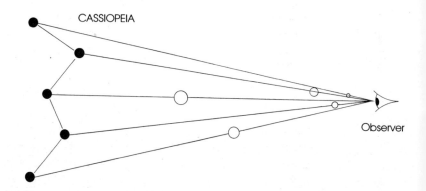

As seen from Great Britain, some constellations never set below the northern horizon. These are *circumpolar* groups and include Cassiopeia together with the bright stars of Ursa Major. Others are visible during certain seasons only, when the night side of the Earth is pointing to the right direction in space (Figure 5.2).

These seasonal designations are not fixed – if you stay up very late on a winter night you will eventually see the spring constellations rising in the east. This motion across the sky is due to the Earth's rotation, while seasonal visibility is caused by the changing position of the Earth in its orbit round the Sun.

Plate 1   The Earth from space

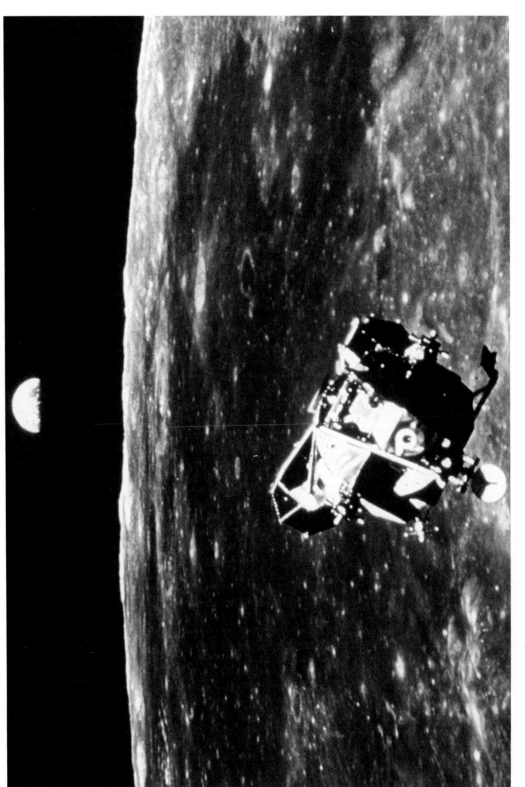

Plate 2   Earthrise from 100 kilometres above the Moon, with the *Apollo* lunar module in the foreground

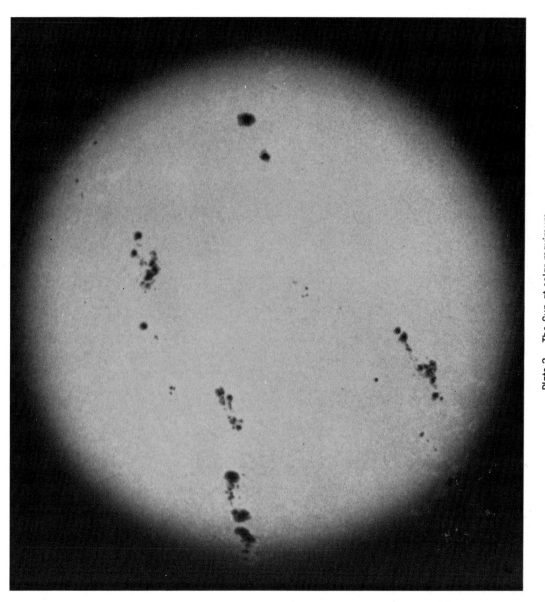

Plate 3　The Sun at solar maximum

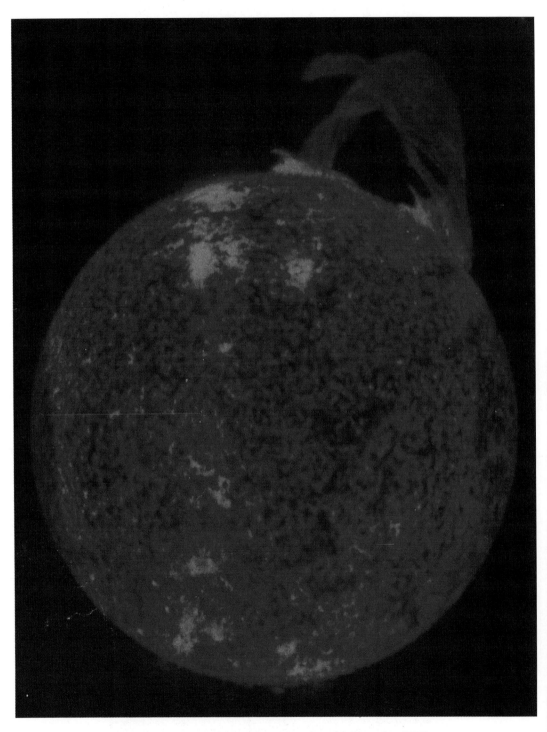

Plate 4   A giant solar eruption observed on 19 December 1973

Plate 5   The surface of Mercury

Plate 6   Cloud patterns in Venus' atmosphere, photographed in
ultraviolet light

Plate 7   The surface of Mars

Plate 8 Intricate patterns in Jupiter's cloud tops, and the satellites Io and Europa (photographed from *Voyager 1*)

Plate 9   Saturn photographed from *Voyager 2*

Plate 10   Saturn's rings show their true splendour in this colour-enhanced
photograph from *Voyager 2*

Plate 11   Uranus' satellite Miranda, with its complex surface features

Plate 12   Comet Ikeya-Seki

Plate 13   The Horse Head Nebula in Orion

Plate 14   The Rosette Nebula with its cluster of young stars

Plate 15   A supernova remnant – the Crab Nebula

Plate 16   A globular cluster visible in the southern hemisphere

Plate 17   The Great Spiral Galaxy in Andromeda

Plate 18   A cluster of galaxies

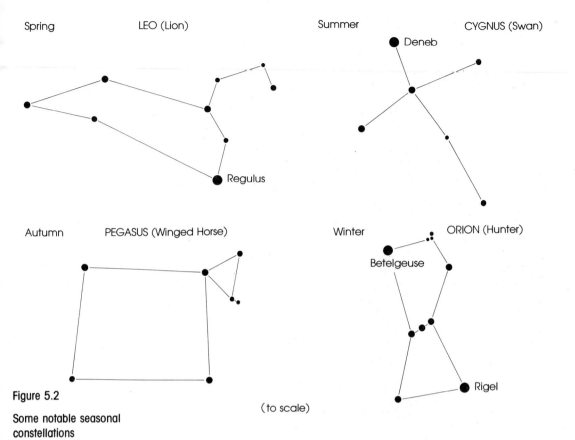

Figure 5.2

Some notable seasonal constellations

ACTIVITY 5

Looking for constellations

Go out on the next clear evening and try to find one of the circumpolar constellations mentioned (either Cassiopeia or Ursa Major) and one seasonal group to suit the time of year. Do not look near street lights!

Wear warm clothes, as even in summer you can get cold standing still looking at the night sky. You do not have to freeze to enjoy the constellations! You might not be successful at first, as the size of constellations relative to the wide areas of sky on view must be learnt. If you were successful, did the constellations appear as you expected them to? Could you see more stars later on?

ACTIVITY 6

Drawing constellations

Try to draw the bright stars in one circumpolar group and a seasonal group without looking at a star map of any kind. Try to get the angles and relative distances between stars correct; do not worry about brightness for now. You may find a *red* torch, pencil and white card useful here (the red light will not ruin your 'night vision'). Finally compare your result with a star chart.

MULTIPLE STARS

Some pairs or groups of stars represent 'real' associations. Only 15% or so of stars are solitary, the others being part of *binary systems, multiples* or *clusters,* in which two or more stars are bound together by gravity. Most pairs which appear close together in the sky are true binaries, though some appear so because they are in nearly the same line of sight. One well-known double star containing stars names Mizar and Alcor can be seen in the 'tail' of the Great Bear, Ursa Major (Figure 5.3).

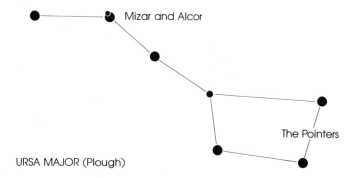

Figure 5.3

The position of Mizar and Alcor in Ursa Major, an *optical double*

There are many examples where hundreds, thousands, and up to a million or more stars have formed together in the same region of space. These *star clusters* will be looked at in Chapter 6. They are very attractive indeed when situated in the Milky Way and viewed with binoculars or a telescope.

BRIGHTNESS

One feature obvious from a glance at the night sky is the variation in brightness among the stars. However, we cannot be sure whether a particular star appears bright because it really is very luminous (and can be seen from a great distance) or whether it is an ordinary star which is nearby; at twice the distance it would be four times fainter.

The apparent brightness of stars was put on a numerical scale of *magnitude* by Hipparchus in the second century BC, and refined by Pogson in 1850. Originally, the brightest stars were said to be of first magnitude, with those just visible to the unaided eye labelled as sixth magnitude. When the system was standardised, some stars were found to be so bright they required negative magnitudes. In reckoning the brightness from apparent magnitude, remember that the smaller the number the brighter the star appears and that this is not necessarily a measure of its true brilliance.

Apparent magnitudes for some stars, with Solar System objects listed for comparison. Note the enormous range of brightness between astronomical objects.

Object	Apparent magnitude
Faintest naked eye star	6.0
Polaris	2.0
Rigel (Orion)	0.1
Sirius	−1.5
Venus	−4.4
Full Moon	−12.7
Sun	−26.7

Careful observation of some stars shows that their brightness is not constant, but you would have to be eagle-eyed (and very patient) to spot the change unless you knew about it beforehand! (This variation is *not* the twinkling which stars show, which is caused by the Earth's atmosphere.) There are several causes: some stars pulsate and change in brightness regularly every few days. Others vary regularly but over much longer periods, while some are binary stars which vary due to eclipses. The table below lists some examples of these types of variable; there are many others.

Some examples of variable stars

Type	Example	
Cepheid	Delta Cephei	(Cepheus)
Long Period	Mira Ceti	(Cetus)
Eclipsing Binary	Algol	(Perseus)

Certain stars are much less predictable, and among these the most spectacular types are the *novae* and *supernovae*. The names mean 'new (star)' and indicate that in many cases the increase in brightness is so great that a previously invisible, faint star flares up to become among the brightest in the sky. The difference between the two types was not appreciated until quite recently. We now think that novae rise in brightness by a factor of one million or so, while supernovae represent a one hundred thousand million-fold increase. With such a difference you might wonder how the confusion could arise – the reason lies in the distance to the star undergoing the change. A supernova at a great distance can resemble a nova (nearby) in terms of apparent brightness.

In either case, the cause of such a dramatic event must be violent and sudden. A nova is believed to occur when nuclear explosions cause one star in a binary system to brighten rapidly, while a supernova explosion involves the 'death' of either a very massive supergiant star or a very small, very dense white dwarf star (see p. 70).

COLOURED STARS

Our eyes cannot see colour well in low light levels and most stars appear white, although a few of the brightest give a hint of colour. Two stars in Orion do this – Rigel can appear blue/white while Betelgeuse is distinctly orange/red. Perhaps the best display of colour is in a telescope view of Albireo, a binary in Cygnus. The components are golden yellow and blue, and the contrast presents a delightful sight. Figure 5.4 shows the location of these stars.

Figure 5.4

Where to locate stars which show colour (a) to the unaided eye, in Orion (the Hunter) and (b) in a telescope, in Cygnus (the Swan). Colours can be seen more often in star trails on colour photographs taken with a time exposure

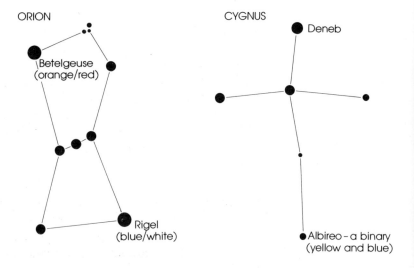

Colour is an indication of the surface temperature of a star. The hottest appear blue while the coolest are red. The following table gives the colour and corresponding surface temperature for a selection of bright stars.

Colour and temperature of some stars

Colour	Surface temperature (degrees Celsius)
Red	2500
Orange	4000
Yellow	6000
White	10 000
Blue	35 000

Like people, stars come in many types and sizes. Some are large, hot and enjoy a relatively short but active existence, while others have a longer but less spectacular life. We think we know all about people, but what exactly *is* a star? Some vital statistics for stars are listed below. For a single star its *mass* is important in shaping its life ahead. In binaries more complex events may occur.

Some vital statistics for stars (see also Figure 5.6)

	Maximum	*Minimum*
Mass	50 solar masses	0.1 solar masses
Luminosity	1 million × Sun's luminosity	0.0001 × Sun's luminosity
Radius	1000 × Sun's radius	0.01 × Sun's radius
Surface temperature	80 000 degrees Celsius	2000 degrees Celsius
Lifetime	1 million million years	1 million years

STAR FORMATION

A star forms out of a large cloud of gas and dust in space, mostly hydrogen, which collapses under gravity to higher densities and higher pressures. Eventually it becomes hot enough to give out light. A steady state is reached when *nuclear fusion* begins in the star's core. The outward pressure from this nuclear furnace eventually balances the inward gravitational pull on the star's outer layers, and a period of stability begins (Figure 5.5). The length of this period depends on the mass of the star. Large pressures and high temperatures are needed to support the outer layers of massive stars. At these higher temperatures the star 'burns' its nuclear fuel more quickly, so massive stars have the shortest lifetimes.

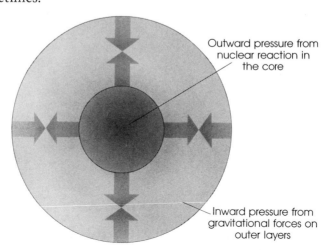

Figure 5.5

The balance of forces in a star

Outward pressure from nuclear reaction in the core

Inward pressure from gravitational forces on outer layers

During the stable phase, hydrogen is being converted into helium at temperatures of around 12 000 000 degrees Celsius or more in the core. Beyond the stability of hydrogen fusion lies a period of more frequent change, with the possibility of further nuclear reactions at the core and in shells surrounding it. High mass stars can produce elements as heavy as iron. Beyond this, fusion does not release energy and the star's life is nearly at an end.

Two possible evolutionary pathways are shown in Figure 5.6, one for a star of the same mass as the Sun, the other for one ten times as massive. In each case the star evolves into a huge red giant, the massive star much more quickly. From there, the pathways diverge. Massive stars end their lives as *neutron stars* or *black holes*, others as white dwarfs.

Figure 5.6

Stages in the life of a solar mass (M⊙) star and a ten solar mass (10 M⊙) star

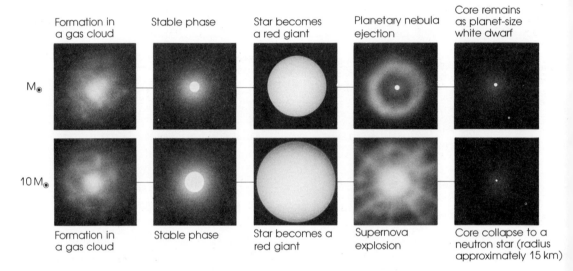

During a star's lifetime, whether it is ten million years or ten thousand million, new chemical elements are produced. In the later stages of evolution this processed material is ejected into space, contributing to the gas and dust which will eventually form new stars. Our planet Earth and the creatures on it are rich in elements produced by stars – so you can rightly claim to be star material!

Populations

The first stars formed from material lacking in the heavier elements, as there could not have been a past generation of stars to produce them. These are known as *population III* stars. Their younger second-generation counterparts will contain a little processed material richer in heavy elements, and these are termed *population II*. The very youngest stars are called *population I*.

HOW FAR ARE THE STARS?

All stars (except the Sun) are so far away that they appear as tiny points of light with no surface detail discernible using direct observation. They are enormous objects, but they lie at great distances. One method for determining this distance for 'nearby' stars depends on an effect known as *parallax*. It can be demonstrated quite simply: hold a finger up at arms length and look at it through one eye only. Note what lies behind it. Now, without moving your finger, close the first eye and open the other. The position of your finger will appear to shift, because of the different viewing positions. In applying this method to observations of stars, the two viewpoints are provided by the changing position of the Earth in its orbit as shown in Figure 5.7(b).

Figure 5.7

Parallax as demonstrated using (a) binocular vision and (b) as used by astronomers to determine the distance to stars

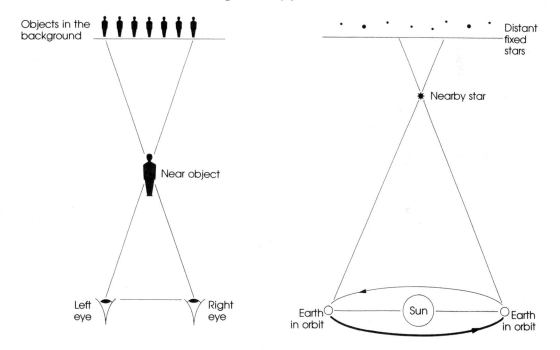

Objects in the background

Near object

Left eye

Right eye

Distant fixed stars

Nearby star

Earth in orbit

Sun

Earth in orbit

By measuring the extremely small shift in the position of a nearby star as viewed at six-monthly intervals, trigonometry can be used to calculate its distance. The unit of distance which arises naturally with this method is the *parsec*; 1 parsec is equal to 3.26 light-years. Remembering that 1 light-year is approximately 9.6 million million kilometres (6 million million miles), the vast scale of our own small neighbourhood in space becomes apparent. Our desire to reach for the stars will not be easy to fulfil. The nearest star, Proxima Centauri, lies at a distance of 1.3 parsecs (4.3 light-years). At a sedate 80 000 kilometres per hour (50 000 miles per hour) the journey would only take 60 000 years, give or take a few hundred!

SUGGESTIONS FOR PROJECTS

1 Throughout the course of one year, learn to recognise and draw the following constellations:

Ursa Major (including use of the Pointers to find Polaris), Taurus, Gemini, Perseus, Auriga, Leo, Virgo, Hercules, Cygnus, Lyra, Pegasus, Andromeda, Cassiopeia (northern hemisphere).

Constellations well placed for observers in the southern hemisphere include Sagittarius, Corona Australis, Scorpius, Norma, Centaurus, Vela, Carina, Puppis, Mensa, Hydra, Musca, Octans.

2 Construct a star chart on card, listing the main constellations only.

QUESTIONS

1 Name one circumpolar constellation and one visible in winter only. Draw the star pattern for each.

2 What are the 12 Zodiacal constellations? Do they deserve special consideration? Discuss the relationship between astrology and astronomy, in today's world and in the past.

3 During naked eye observation of the constellations from a dark site, an astronomer notices that she can see more stars after 20 minutes' observation than at the start. Why is this? Design a *safe* experiment to test your ideas.

4 Place the following objects in order of increasing brightness, and say which would be visible to the unaided eye.

Object	Apparent magnitude
Pluto	14.0
Sirius	−1.5
Polaris	2.0
Neptune	7.7

5 Two stars have 2 and 15 solar masses. Which will have the longest lifetime? Population III stars may have had masses greater than one hundred solar masses. If so, would any remain in existence today?

CONSTELLATIONS

The view from Earth of the constellations will change over long periods of time due to the *proper motion* of their constituent stars (Figure 5.8). Proper motion is the annual apparent shift of a star on the sky due to its motion through space; usually this positional change is imperceptible over centuries, but occasionally a nearby star has a large proper motion. One such case is *Barnard's Star*. Photographs taken only a few tens of years apart clearly show its shift against the background patterns of 'fixed' stars.

Figure 5.8

Present and future appearance of Cassiopeia – the differences are due to the proper motion of each star

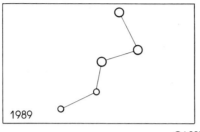 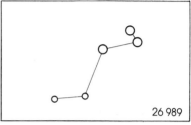

1989   26 989

CASSIOPEIA

The arbitrary nature of the constellations becomes more apparent when vantage points other than spaceship Earth are considered. From nearby Alpha Centauri, Cassiopeia would appear much the same as always, but with the addition of one extra bright star – the Sun!

MAGNITUDE: A NUMERICAL SCALE DEFINED

The *apparent magnitude* of a star depends on the amount of light it emits and its distance from the observer. On the scale used today, a difference of 5 magnitudes corresponds to a 100-fold ratio in brightness. This gives an increase in brightness by a factor of 2.51 for every unit difference in magnitude. (2.51 is the fifth root of 100.)

The relationship between magnitude differences and apparent brightness

Difference in magnitude	Ratio of apparent brightness
1	2.51
2	$2.51 \times 2.51 = 6.30$
3	$(2.51)^3 = 15.81$
5	$(2.51)^5 = 100.0$

Calculations on the relationship between the difference in apparent magnitude of two stars (m_1 and m_2) and their apparent brightness (b_1 and b_2) can be carried out using *Pogson's formula*:

$$m_1 - m_2 = 2.5 \log_{10} \frac{b_2}{b_1}$$

The true luminosity of a star depends on its size (surface area) and effective temperature. Luminosity is expressed in watts

(1 watt = 1 joule per second); our Sun has a power output of approximately 4×10^{26} W, which is modest by stellar standards. If the *absolute magnitude* of a star is to be found, the effect of distance must be taken into account.

TRIGONOMETRIC PARALLAX

In this method of distance determination, the parallax angle (π) for a star is found by observing from two points, one at each end of a baseline provided by the diameter of the Earth's orbit as shown in Figure 5.9.

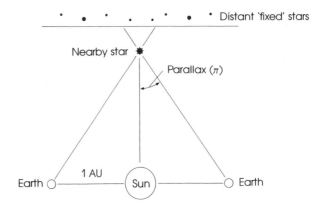

Figure 5.9

Determining distance using measurements of the annual parallax angle (π)

When a star has a parallax of 1 second of arc $\left(\dfrac{1°}{3600}\right)$ it is defined to be at a distance of 1 parsec (abbreviation pc; 1 pc is equal to 3.26 light-years). In general the distance d in parsecs to a star with annual parallax π is given by

$$d = \frac{1}{\pi}$$

Annual parallax values for stars are extremely small. The nearest star (Proxima Centauri) has a value for π of 0.76 seconds of arc, which corresponds to a distance of just less than 1.32 parsecs. Beyond 100 parsecs the method becomes unreliable.

Once the distance to a star is known, from parallax or another suitable method, its absolute magnitude can be calculated. This is the apparent magnitude a star would have if observed from the standard distance of 10 parsecs. Absolute magnitudes give a true picture of relative luminosity; some examples are given below.

Apparent and absolute magnitudes for three stars

Star	Apparent magnitude	Absolute magnitude
Sun	−26.7	+4.8
Rigel	+0.1	−7.1
Proxima Centauri	+11.0	+15.4

CEPHEID VARIABLES

One particular class of variable star useful in distance determination is the *Cepheid* class, named after the prototype Delta Cephei. These stars vary in luminosity in a regular manner over periods of a few days, but their range is not great, typically less than 1 magnitude. Cepheids, large, luminous stars which vary in brightness as they expand and contract, were shown to be useful in distance determination following work by Henrietta Leavitt in 1912. She found that the period of a Cepheid is related to its absolute magnitude (longer periods imply larger absolute magnitudes). With the distance to some nearby Cepheids determined by an independent method, a calibrated scale was established to find the distance to other such variables with known period. Refined versions of this method can be used for stars at great distances.

ECLIPSING BINARIES

If the Earth happens to lie along the plane of the orbit of a binary system, the stars will be seen to pass in front of each other periodically. Although the two stars may lie too close together to be seen separately, the total brightness of the 'single' star will vary – this is shown in Figure 5.10 together with the *light curve*.

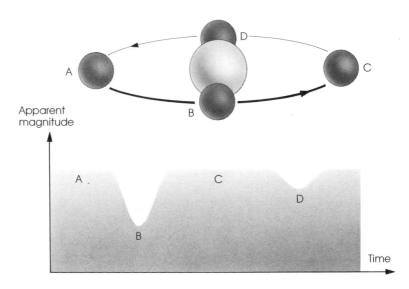

Figure 5.10

The light curve for an eclipsing binary. The two stars actually orbit around their centre of mass, but the view can be simplified by considering the motion of one component relative to its companion

The first star of this type to be discovered was Algol in Perseus. The mass of the member stars in this and similar systems can be calculated from observations of the orbit.

LONG-PERIOD VARIABLES

These stars vary over a few magnitudes with periods typically of a few hundred days. They are usually noticeably red in colour, as they are highly luminous red giants (see p. 69). The famous star Mira Ceti is an example of this class, varying between magnitude 3 (visible to the naked eye) and magnitude 10 (invisible to the naked eye). Like Cepheids, these stars appear to pulsate.

CLASSIFYING STARS: THE HERTZSPRUNG–RUSSELL DIAGRAM

If you were to plot a graph of mass (or weight) against height for 20 or so people (say a class) you would get results similar to Figure 5.11.

The points lie around a straight line, not on one. We can say that there is a *correlation* between a person's weight and their height. Some individuals will be well away from the line corresponding to Mr or Miss Average.

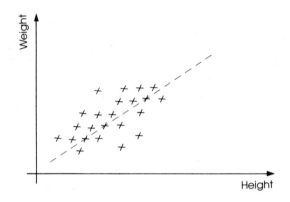

Figure 5.11

The correlation between height and weight for a number of people

A similar correlation for stars developed in the early part of the twentieth century by H. N. Russell and E. Hertzsprung has been invaluable in guiding the thoughts of astronomers on stellar evolution. When luminosity (absolute magnitude) is plotted against effective temperature (or colour) many stars lie around a diagonal line known as the *main sequence* (see Figure 5.12).

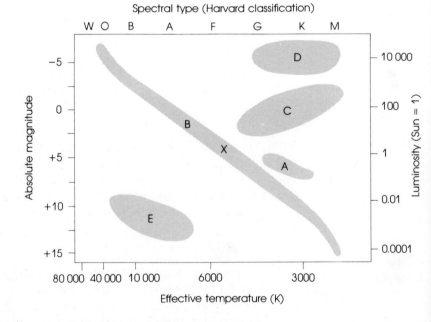

Figure 5.12

A Hertzsprung–Russell (HR) diagram. Note that temperature increases to the left, and that most stars lie on a diagonal line running from top left to bottom right (the main sequence)

Key
A T-Tauri variables   C Red giants   E White dwarfs
B Main sequence   D Supergiants   X Sun

The diagonal position of the main sequence is reasonably easy to understand, as hot stars should be more luminous. But luminosity varies with surface area as well as temperature, so we should not be surprised to find cool stars which are luminous because of their great size (the red giants), and very hot stars which are faint because they are so small (the white dwarfs).

At first the main sequence was thought to represent an evolutionary pathway, which stars enter as hot blue objects at the top left (after forming as red giants) then move down to the bottom right as they cool. This is incorrect; the main sequence is now known to represent the stable phase of hydrogen fusion, with a star's position on it determined by mass. The evolutionary pathways for a star of mass equal to the Sun ($M_\odot$) and one ten times as massive ($10M_\odot$) are thought to be as shown in the HR diagrams (Figure 5.13(a) and (b)); compare this with Figure 5.6 on p. 62.

Figure 5.13

Tracks in the HR diagram traced by two stars, one of mass $M_\odot$ the other $10M_\odot$ ((a) and (b) respectively) as they evolve

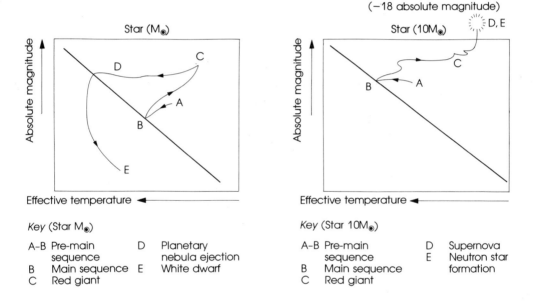

Key (Star $M_\odot$)

A-B	Pre-main sequence	D	Planetary nebula ejection
B	Main sequence	E	White dwarf
C	Red giant		

Key (Star $10M_\odot$)

A-B	Pre-main sequence	D	Supernova
B	Main sequence	E	Neutron star formation
C	Red giant		

STAR DEATH

The ultimate fate of an old star also depends on its mass. If this ends up as less than about 1.4 times the mass of the Sun, the star will be able to fade quietly as a white dwarf. Many such stars have been identified, a notable example being the companion to Sirius, Sirius B. White dwarf matter is extremely dense; 1 cubic centimetre would have a mass of about 1000 kilograms (1 tonne).

Above this *Chandrasekhar limiting mass*, a star's core will collapse to even higher densities and become a *neutron star*. The density of neutron stars is truly immense, with 1 cubic centimetre of material corresponding to a mass of around 1 000 000 000 tonnes! The first identification of such an object was by Jocelyn Bell at Cambridge, England, in 1967,

Figure 5.14

Pulsars send out a
beam of radiation,
which sweeps round
as the pulsar rotates

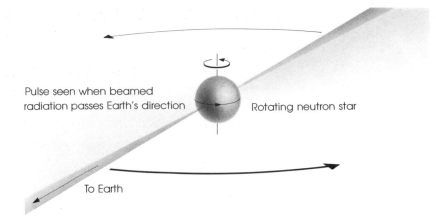

Pulse seen when beamed
radiation passes Earth's direction

Rotating neutron star

To Earth

although its nature was not immediately recognised. These
pulsating radio sources (*pulsars*) discovered at Cambridge were
finally identified as *rotating* neutron stars, which beam radiation,
like a lighthouse, into space (Figure 5.14).

There is also a limit to the mass of a stable neutron star, which
lies between 2 and 3 solar masses. Beyond this, further collapse
will ultimately produce a *black hole* (see below). White dwarf
stars remain after planetary nebula ejection (see Figure 5.6 and
p. 69), while neutron stars and black holes may be formed in
supernova explosions.

NOVAE AND SUPERNOVAE

Novae are believed to occur when mass transfer on to a white
dwarf in a binary system leads to runaway nuclear reactions near
its surface. The outburst is less energetic than a supernova event
and can recur at intervals in the same binary system.

There are two main types of supernovae, characterised by their
light curve and spectrum. *Type I* supernovae occur in binary
systems in which one component is a white dwarf, while *type II*
events involve a highly evolved massive star which undergoes
core collapse after exhausting its supplies of nuclear fuel. The
amount of energy released in the subsequent explosion is vast,
exceeding the total output of the Sun in its entire lifetime. A
neutron star (pulsar) or black hole may be left behind in the
supernova remnant, within material ejected at 80 000 000
kilometres per hour! During the explosion, heavy elements such
as gold are produced.

BLACK HOLES

A collapsed object becomes a black hole when the escape
velocity from a region of space around it exceeds the speed of
light. Black holes are invisible, so the problem of detecting them
rests with observing binary systems in which one object is
invisible and where observations of the visible component imply
a mass for its companion above the limit for a neutron star.
Such a system would be expected to emit X-rays, and a

promising candidate is the X-ray source Cygnus X-1, which fulfils these criteria. Figure 5.15 shows a representation of such a system.

Black holes are exotic and controversial objects; once very fashionable in explaining many obscure phenomena, some scientists now find it difficult to accept that matter can be crushed out of existence by the infinite forces at their centres.

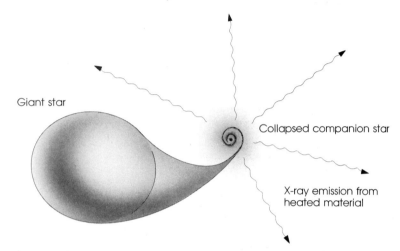

Figure 5.15

Mass transfer onto a collapsed star – an X-ray binary

Giant star

Collapsed companion star

X-ray emission from heated material

SUGGESTIONS FOR PROJECTS

3 Choose a constellation (preferably a large one) and observe it in detail. Estimate the magnitude (and colour where possible) of stars in it using comparisons you have looked up beforehand on a star chart or atlas.

4 Using a camera on a tripod, loaded with fast colour slide film for simplicity, take an exposure of the sky around Polaris of at least 40 minutes duration. Use a cable release to avoid camera shake on exposure, wait for a dark night with long clear periods and time the exposure accurately. Use the slides (take at least two photographs) to calculate the time taken for the Earth to rotate relative to the stars. Look for satellite trails and note any colours shown by stars.

5 Using star chart magnitudes for comparison, observe Algol or another eclipsing binary and draw the light curve. (Minima occur at intervals of 2.8 days and last for 20 minutes.) It would be very interesting to compare the light curve of Algol with that of Beta Lyrae, which is situated near the brilliant star Vega in Lyra. Beta Lyrae varies over 12 day intervals. Algol is an autumn and winter object, while Beta Lyrae is visible in summer.

QUESTIONS

6 (a) What is the difference between apparent magnitude and absolute magnitude?
   (b) Calculate the difference in apparent magnitude between two stars, one of which is 5 times brighter than the other.

7 How far away must a star be to give an annual parallax of 0.2 seconds of arc?

8 Describe the use of Cepheid variables in distance determination.

9 A main sequence star of less than 8 solar masses may be able to lose enough mass to end its life as a white dwarf. How much mass must a 5 solar mass star lose to become a stable white dwarf?

10 If a supernova event produces a visible supernova remnant and a pulsar, give two reasons why the pulsar may not be observable in the remnant as seen from Earth.

11 Lines can be drawn across the HR diagram linking stars of approximately equal radius. In which direction should these lines be drawn?

6

THE GALAXY

THE MILKY WAY

On a clear night, when looking at Cygnus from a dark site, a broad band of faint light will become visible stretching through the constellation and on towards the horizon on either side. Southern hemisphere observers have an even better view of the *Milky Way* when looking at Sagittarius. With the invention of the telescope, this glow was shown to be a collection of faint stars packed closely together. What you are doing in looking at the Milky Way is observing our own Galaxy from within (Note: we use a capital G in Galaxy, when referring to the Milky Way.) All the stars in the sky are members of the Milky Way.

Figure 6.1

The stars of the Milky Way photographed from Australia

Our Sun is one of about one hundred thousand million stars in the Galaxy. Seen from outside, edge on, the Galaxy would look like a thin oval with a slightly fatter central region. From above, it would appear circular with a spiral pattern (see Figure 6.2, on the next page).

A galaxy is a 'star city', a collection of stars drifting through space, bound by gravity, and our own Milky Way is thought to be a typical example of a *spiral* galaxy. The true shape and size of the Galaxy, and our position within it, has taken many years to establish and is still the subject of debate.

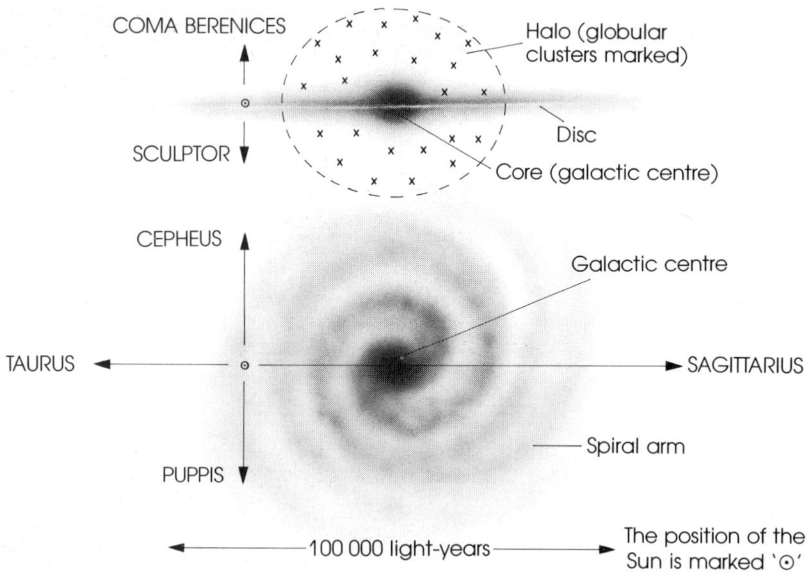

Figure 6.2

The appearance of the Milky Way from two vantage points outside. The approximate dimensions are shown, together with the position of the Sun

OBJECTS IN THE MILKY WAY

Many of the objects in our skies are too faint to be seen with the unaided eye. Most are linked to the life cycle of stars, and *can* be seen with binoculars or a small telescope.

DARK NEBULAE

The light from the Milky Way is not uniform in brightness – there are many dark patches and lanes which seem to be empty of stars. These are due to large clouds of cold, dark dust and gas blocking the light from more distant stars in the background. These clouds (*nebulae*) block starlight so efficiently that our view into the stars of the Milky Way is very limited, and we cannot see the centre of the Galaxy.

Two well-known examples are the 'Horse Head' Nebula in Orion (Plate 13) and the 'Coal Sack' in Crux Australis (Figure 6.3, on the opposite page). Both are more readily appreciated from photographs than by direct observation.

These dark clouds consist largely of hydrogen, with other atoms and molecules such as carbon and carbon monoxide. They represent the earliest stage of star formation in that they contain the raw materials from which stars will be made. Collapse into stars may be caused by compression as the material enters a dense spiral arm, or by shock waves from a nearby supernova explosion. The result may be a single star, a binary, a multiple star or a cluster.

Figure 6.3

The Coal Sack, an
example of a dark
nebula

BRIGHT NEBULAE

As part of a gas cloud collapses, the radiation emitted by a
young star will at first be blocked by the surrounding cold
material. Eventually the radiation will become sufficiently
intense to cause the surrounding gas to glow, producing a
bright *emission nebula*. One such nebula visible to the unaided
eye is the Great Nebula in Orion (Figure 6.4), situated below
the Hunter's prominent belt of three stars.

As young stars begin to shine, the flow of particles and
radiation away from their surfaces halts the influx of material
from the collapsing cloud and may create a cavity within the
nebula (Plate 14).

Figure 6.4

Gaseous nebulae are
the birthplace of stars.
The Great Nebula in
Orion: at its heart is a
cluster of hot young
stars which cause the
nebula to glow. The
red colour seen in
colour photographs
shows the presence
of hydrogen

OPEN STAR CLUSTERS

Large clouds of gas can collapse to produce clusters of stars, which may contain anything from a handful of members to over a thousand. These *open clusters* (Figure 6.5) are scattered across the Milky Way and many are magnificent sights in a telescope. We see the brightest members, which are mostly young blue/white stars with the occasional 'heavyweight' which has evolved to add a touch of red to the scene.

There are very few old open clusters. As their membership is limited, they cannot withstand the gravitational tug-of-war between stars within the cluster and other objects in the Galaxy. Those which survive disruption the longest are either situated out of the plane of the Milky Way, where the chances of being disturbed are less, or have more member stars than usual – or both.

Some open clusters have wisps of nebulosity visible nearby, the remains of the nebula from which they formed. These *reflection nebulae* 'shine' by scattering the starlight from cluster members. Blue light scatters well, so reflection nebulae appear blue in colour photographs.

(a)

Figure 6.5

(a) A rich open cluster in the constellation Auriga. (b) A nearby cluster, the famous Pleiades in Taurus are easily visible to the unaided eye

(b)

PLANETARY NEBULAE

The name *planetary nebula* can be rather confusing as such an object is not a planet, nor a nebula in the ordinary sense. Planetary nebulae represent the decline into old age of a low-mass star, and are formed when the outer layers of a red giant are puffed off into space. This leaves behind a small stellar core which has a high surface temperature – a shell of expanding gas surrounding a white dwarf is an apt description of a planetary nebula.

Appearances differ from one planetary nebula to another (Figure 6.6). Some have ring structures like the famous Ring Nebula, while others have a small evenly illuminated disc. This gave rise to their name, as such objects resembled the small disc of the planets as seen by observers in the past.

(a)

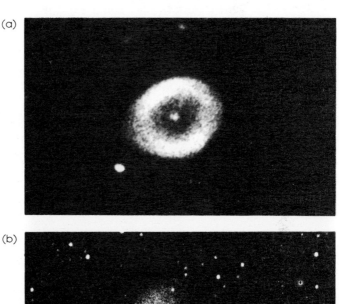

Figure 6.6

Two famous planetary nebulae: (a) the Ring Nebula in Lyra and (b) the Dumb-bell Nebula in Vulpecula. Note the central star in each

(b)

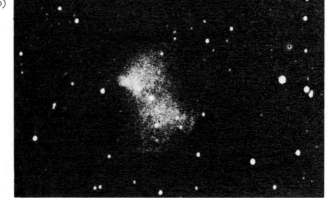

Those planetary nebulae which form in our galactic neighbourhood will remain visible for little more than a hundred thousand years. As the gases expand and cool they will eventually disappear from view. Also, planetary nebula formation will not take place with more massive stars, which are destined for a more dramatic finale as supernovae.

SUPERNOVA REMNANTS

When energy production from nuclear fusion in the core of a massive star stops, there is an implosion followed by an explosion. This throws off a rapidly expanding shell of material and releases an enormous amount of energy which we see as a supernova. Depending on the mass of the star, and the amount of material lost during the later stages of evolution, the core may collapse into a neutron star or black hole. As the ejected material expands, it becomes observable as a *supernova remnant*.

Not all supernovae leave behind a collapsed star. Some supernovae are believed to involve runaway nuclear reactions which disrupt an entire white dwarf star, rendered unstable by mass transfer from a companion in a binary system.

One example of a filled supernova remnant is the Crab Nebula, formed during the outburst recorded by Chinese astronomers on 4 July 1054 as an extremely bright 'new star' in Taurus. The Crab contains a rapidly rotating neutron star – a pulsar — and is shown in Figure 6.7 (see also Plate 15) together with an older remnant, the Veil Nebula in Cygnus.

In a typical galaxy, supernovae occur every 30 years or so, but in our Galaxy many remain hidden behind dark nebulae in the Milky Way. Another visible supernova in our Galaxy is overdue, the last having occurred in 1604. However, a supernova was seen in a nearby galaxy, the Large Magellanic Cloud, in 1987, and became a bright, naked-eye object.

Figure 6.7

(a) The Crab Nebula and (b) the Veil Nebula, two supernova remnants. Their tortured appearance reflects the violence of their birth

(a)

(b)

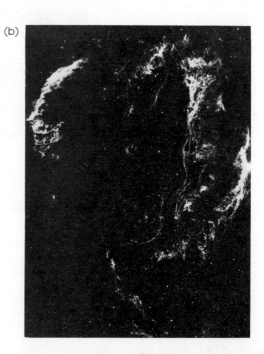

GLOBULAR CLUSTERS

The objects covered so far are to be found in the Galaxy's spiral arms, where star formation occurs. *Globular clusters* (Plate 16), however, are situated well out of the galactic disc. They are very concentrated groups of up to a million stars, larger than their open cluster cousins, stable and much older – globular cluster stars may have been among the first to form in the Galaxy. Two globulars, the great Hercules cluster and a smaller cluster in Lyra, are shown in Figure 6.8.

(a)

(b)

Figure 6.8

Globular clusters are dense groupings of old stars. These clusters are in the constellations (a) Hercules, and (b) Lyra

There are several hundred globular clusters in a spherical halo centred on the galactic core. This arrangement may be due to the fact that the clusters formed when the Galaxy was approximately spherical in shape, before it became the flattened spiral it is today. Our position in the Milky Way, shown in Figure 6.1, was deduced from observations of the distribution of globular clusters in the sky, which appear to be concentrated in Sagittarius – the home of our Galaxy's hidden centre. Today's powerful telescopes can see globular clusters in similar arrangements around other galaxies.

MORE GALAXIES

The *Magellanic Clouds* (Figure 6.9) are known to be independent star systems, smaller galaxies orbiting our own Milky Way. They show many of the features we see in the Milky Way, and form our nearest neighbours in a universe filled with galaxies. Our Galaxy is not the only star system.

(a)

(b)

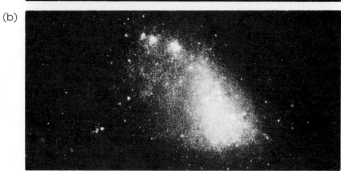

Figure 6.9

The Large (a) and Small (b) Magellanic Clouds, galaxies orbiting the Milky Way. They are visible as nebulous patches to observers in the southern hemisphere

SUGGESTIONS FOR PROJECTS

1 Using the naked eye and binoculars or a telescope (if available) scan the summer and winter Milky Way. Look for open clusters and nebulae as well as the large-scale structure of the star clouds.

2 Use a telescope and star chart to observe and sketch selected *Messier objects* – nebulae, clusters and planetary nebulae. (Such objects were among those catalogued by the French astronomer Charles Messier.)

QUESTIONS

1 List three types of object found in the Milky Way, and briefly explain how they fit into the life cycle of a star.

2 Which type of star, population I or II, would you expect to find in a globular cluster? Explain your answer.

3 If the Ring Nebula (Figure 6.6(a)) is a shell of even thickness, explain why the central portion appears fainter than the edge.

4 How is it that we can observe globular clusters out to 30 000 parsecs (100 000 light-years) and beyond yet the most distant open clusters visible are around 3000 parsecs (10 000 light-years) away?

MAPPING THE GALAXY

It is difficult to draw up a map of the Galaxy, for the simple reason that we live inside it. The first astronomer to give anything like a reasonable picture was William Herschel (1738–1822) who used his telescopes to make 'reviews of the heavens' and carefully counted the stars in various selected areas. From these results, he deducted that the Galaxy is shaped like 'a cloven grindstone', which was not so very far from the truth.

Herschel, naturally, supposed that the Sun must lie at or near the centre of the Galaxy. By observing the tiny movements of stars in different parts of the sky he was able to establish that the Solar System is at present moving towards a point in the constellation Hercules, but this was no clue to our actual position, and neither had Herschel any good idea of the size of the Galaxy.

In our own century, Harlow Shapley made new attempts to measure the size of the Galaxy. He concentrated upon the globular clusters, which, as we have seen, are huge symmetrical systems which are very remote. (Only three are visible with the naked eye: Messier 13 (*M13*) in Hercules, and the far-southern Omega Centauri and 47 Tucanae.) Globular clusters contain short-period variables, which 'give away' their distances by the way in which they behave. The globulars also form a kind of outer framework to the Galaxy, and Shapley's results were remarkably good. We now know that the Galaxy measures approximately 100 000 light-years from one side to the other. This may be a slight over-estimate, but is certainly not very far wrong.

Shapley also realised that the globular clusters are not distributed evenly all over the sky. There are more of them in the southern hemisphere than in the northern, and there is a marked concentration in the region of the southern constellation Sagittarius. In fact, we have a lop-sided view; the Sun is well away from the galactic centre. The distance of the Solar System from the actual centre is of the order of 30 000 light-years (over 9000 parsecs).

RADIO WAVES FROM THE GALAXY

Many of the outer galaxies, such as M31 in Andromeda, are spiral in form, and there seemed to be a good chance that our Galaxy too was spiral. Proof of this came from radio astronomy, which began in the 1930s, though it did not become important until after the end of the Second World War.

Radio waves are collected by 'radio telescopes', which are like large aerials; the most famous of them is the Lovell Telescope, at Jodrell Bank in Cheshire, which is a 'dish' (though it must be stressed that by no means all radio telescopes are dishes) (Figure 9.9(a), p. 107). The clouds of cold hydrogen spread through the Galaxy send out radiations at a wavelength of 21.1 centimetres, so that their positions and velocities can be plotted. It was found that they concentrate in the spiral arms, and that the Galaxy is shaped like a Catherine wheel, with a central 'bulge' and an outer halo, which includes the globular clusters as well as individual stars (see p. 74).

ROTATION OF THE GALAXY

It has been found that the Galaxy is rotating round its centre. The Sun is moving at around 250 kilometres per second, and has a rotation period around the galactic centre of about 225 000 000 years, a period sometimes called the 'cosmic year'. One cosmic year ago, the most advanced life forms on Earth were amphibians; even the dinosaurs had yet to make their appearance. It is interesting to speculate as to what our world will be like one cosmic year hence!

THE MASS OF THE GALAXY

It seems that our Galaxy is slightly above the average in size, though it is by no means exceptional; for instance, the Andromeda Spiral, M31, is decidedly larger and more populous.

The Galaxy contains about one hundred thousand million stars. It is mainly 'space'. If the stars are represented by rice-grains, then to give a good idea of the population density in the Sun's region we would have to fill a wine-glass with rice-grains and then scatter them at random over an area the size of the British Isles.

The mass of the Galaxy can be estimated by studying the movements of the objects which we can see. Remarkably, it seems that although the total mass is about one million million times that of the Sun, this is around ten times the combined mass of all the objects we can see – stars, clusters, nebulae and everything else. There is a tremendous amount of 'hidden mass', and at present its nature remains unknown.

THE SPIRAL ARMS

The origin of spiral arms is uncertain. There are apparently 'density waves' which are rotating; in these density waves, star formation is triggered off, and spiral arms result. It is not likely

Figure 6.10

A galaxy does not rotate like a gramophone record. The inner regions rotate more quickly, and this will cause a spiral pattern to 'wind up' and, eventually, disappear. In this schematic diagram of a rotating galaxy, regions of stars in the original spiral arm are shown as shaded dots

that any particular arm is a permanent feature, otherwise the arms would tend to 'wind up' as the Galaxy rotates (Figure 6.10).

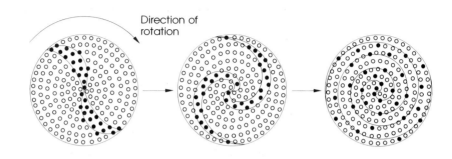

Direction of rotation

THE LOCAL GROUP

Our Galaxy is a member of what is termed the local group, of which the other principal members are the Andromeda Spiral (M31), the smaller Triangulum Spiral (M33) and the two Magellanic Clouds, plus possibly an elliptical system, Maffei 1, about which we know little because it is so heavily obscured by material in the main plane of our own Galaxy.

The local group also contains more than 20 dwarf systems, some of which are not a great deal larger than major globular clusters (see Chapter 7).

SUGGESTIONS FOR PROJECTS

3 Make a model of the Galaxy, using wire and cotton wool and mark the approximate position of the Sun.

4 Photograph the summer or winter Milky Way using a camera mounted on a tripod, a cable shutter release and fast film (at least 400 ASA/ISO). Wait for a night with no atmospheric haze and try exposures of between 15 seconds and 1 minute. (For long exposures, set the shutter to 'B'.)

QUESTIONS

5 How was the Sun's position in our Galaxy deduced?

6 If the Sun was situated well out of the plane of the Galaxy, how would our view of the Milky Way differ?

7 On a scale where 1 astronomical unit is 1 inch, what is the scaled distance between:
(a) the Sun and Pluto?
(b) two stars in the Galaxy which are 4 light-years apart?
(c) the Sun and the Galactic centre?

(Note: the number of astronomical units in 1 light-year is approximately equal to the number of inches in 1 mile.)

CHAPTER 7

THE DISTANT UNIVERSE

SPIRAL NEBULAE

Until 1920, the true nature of 'spiral nebulae' was uncertain. Some astronomers thought that they were relatively nearby in our Galaxy, while others believed them to be much more distant. The diameter of the Galaxy had been measured by Harlow Shapley, so if the distance to spiral nebulae could be found, their position inside or outside the Galaxy would be known. But were they gas or stars?

Spiral form had been recognised in some nebulae since a drawing produced by the Earl of Rosse in 1845, but final identification had to wait for the construction of a 2.5-metre (100-inch) reflector at Mount Wilson, California. With this telescope, individual stars including Cepheid variables, could be resolved in spiral nebulae. In spite of some confusion between types of Cepheid, use of these stars to find distance (p. 67) showed that even the largest (and therefore nearest) spiral nebulae were too far away to be inside our own Galaxy. The distance to the nearest major spiral galaxy, visible to the unaided eye in Andromeda (Figure 7.1), is now estimated to be 675 000 parsecs (2 200 000 light-years). Spiral nebulae are huge star systems.

Figure 7.1

The Great Spiral Galaxy in Andromeda

GALAXIES

Research on galaxies in the 1920s by Edwin Hubble, which proved that they were independent star systems, also produced a classification of galaxies depending on their shape. Hubble recognised several recurring forms – *spirals, barred spirals* and *elliptical galaxies* were noted, together with less symmetrical *irregulars*. When arranged into a 'tuning fork' diagram (Figure 7.2) it is tempting to think of the sequence as representing galactic evolution, with galaxies spinning themselves into a flattened form before disintegrating.

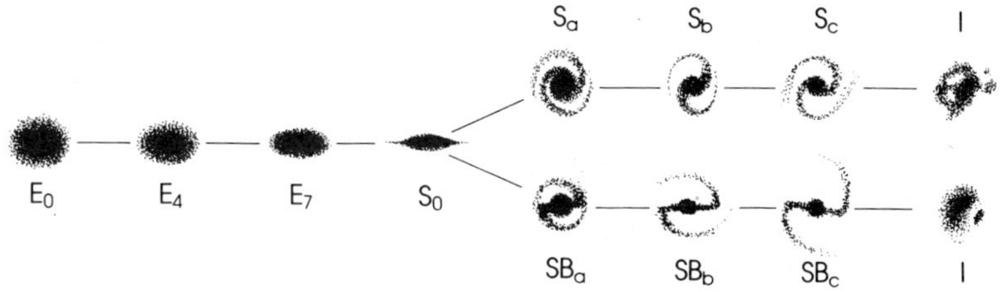

Figure 7.2

A Hubble 'tuning fork' diagram, showing the designations for spiral (S), barred spiral (SB), elliptical (E) and irregular (I) galaxies. Elliptical galaxies are further labelled 0–7 depending on the degree of flattening, while spirals are classed o-a-b-c depending on the relative importance of the core and spiral arms

The classification of a particular galaxy within this system is to some extent dependent on our view of it, and an evolutionary link is now discounted. What we may be seeing in parts of the Hubble diagram is a conservationary sequence: how good the galaxies are at conserving their star-forming material. Most galaxies seem to be roughly the same age (ten thousand million years) but their content varies. Many irregular galaxies, and the arms of spirals, are rich in gas and dust from which stars are forming. They contain many young population I stars (see Plate 17). Elliptical galaxies, together with the cores of spirals, have little or no star-forming material and consist of older population II stars. For some reason, certain galaxy types continue to produce stars for longer than others.

A typical galaxy like our own contains about one hundred thousand million stars, but there are *dwarf* galaxies with only one million members and *giant ellipticals* with populations many times that of an ordinary spiral (see table below).

The size of some galaxies compared to our own

Galaxy type	Mass (Milky Way = 1)
Giant elliptical	10–100
Spiral	1
Small spiral	0.1
Irregular	0.1
Dwarf elliptical	0.00001

THE LOCAL GROUP

With the distance to nearby galaxies established, it became clear that galaxies are not spread evenly through space (Plate 18). Our own galaxy is the lesser of two dominant spirals in a cluster known as the *local group*, the other being the spiral galaxy in Andromeda (Figure 7.1).

The Magellanic Clouds (see Figure 6.9 (p. 80)), visible in the southern hemisphere, are small irregular galaxies which orbit their larger neighbour (our Galaxy) in constant peril from its gravity. A distance of 52 000 parsecs (170 000 light-years) allows close study of the objects within these companions systems.

CLUSTERS OF GALAXIES

The local group is a small cluster of galaxies situated at the outer edge of the *Virgo supercluster*. This arrangement represents one of the large-scale structures of the universe: a galactic supercluster. In contemplating these enormous 'clusters of clusters' we would do well to remind ourselves of the sizes and distances involved.

A typical galaxy is around 30 000 parsecs (100 000 light-years) across, and may be part of a cluster some 15 000 000 parsecs (50 000 000 light-years) in diameter. Superclusters are ten times larger again! How can distances on this scale be estimated?

Where Cepheid variables cannot be identified, brighter objects such as supergiants and emission nebulae often can. By comparison with similar objects in nearby galaxies, the distance to remote objects can be estimated. Supernovae provide another form of 'standard candle'. In these cases, the uncertainty in the distance estimate can reach 50% or more.

To extend measurements even further, astronomers use an effect known as the *red shift* (see below).

THE DOPPLER EFFECT

During Hubble's researches, those galaxies beyond the local group had been shown to be moving away from us. This information came from a study of the *spectrum* of each galaxy, obtained by spreading out the light into its constituent colours using a prism or similar device. Patterns in the spectrum shift position if the galaxy emitting the light is moving towards or away from the observer – an example of the *Doppler effect*. Receding galaxies show patterns displaced towards the red region of the spectrum, hence, red shift. (Nearby galaxies may show a *blue shift* due to internal motions within the local group – the Andromeda Spiral does this.)

The basis of distance determination using this technique is Hubble's law: the velocity of recession of a galaxy (as inferred from its red shift) is proportional to its distance. This relationship has been questioned in recent years.

QUASARS

The objects which have raised doubts over the velocity/ distance relationship are QSOs – *quasi-stellar objects* or *quasars*. Quasars were discovered in 1963 and have the following characteristics:

- They show very high red shifts.
- Their brightness varies over short periods of time.
- They are compact, appearing like stars, but emit huge amounts of energy.

To date, the most distant quasar has a red shift of 4.5 (the higher the number quoted for a red shift, presently 0–4.5, the greater the velocity of recession) which implies a speed of recession 93% of light speed. If the velocity/distance link is true, this object is many *thousands of millions* of light-years away.

Some astronomers dispute the fact that quasars are so far away because of a number of photographs which appear to show a quasar (or quasars), with high red shift, connected to a 'nearby' galaxy with low red shift. If this connection, physical or statistical, is real, then the objects must all be at similar distances. The high quasar red shifts will then require another explanation.

Given that quasars are as distant as Hubble's law suggests, there must be a small but extremely powerful energy source within them. They are believed to be galaxies with very active centres, possibly powered by black holes. We see the 4.5 red shift quasar as it was when the universe was one tenth of its present age.

THE EXPANDING UNIVERSE

The observation that all distant galaxies are moving away suggests that the universe is expanding. Our position is not special – we are not at the centre of the expansion. Other observers in other galaxies would see exactly the same process. To understand this, imagine the surface of a balloon as part of the universe, with galaxies drawn a set distance apart on its surface. As the balloon inflates (as the universe expands) the distance between *any* galaxy and its neighbours increases (Figure 7.3). So all galaxies seem to be the centre of the expansion, but none are!

Tracking this expansion backwards, there must have been a time when the contents of the universe were much closer together.

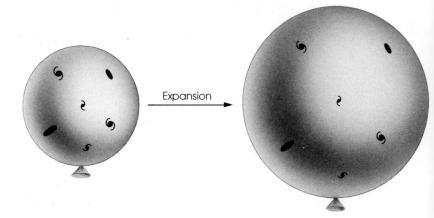

Figure 7.3

A simple model of the expanding universe

Expansion

THE BIG BANG THEORY

In the *hot Big Bang* model of the origin of the universe, the galaxies formed from matter created and expelled following the explosion of a hot, dense fireball. The observed expansion of the universe is then a consequence of this initial explosion. In the explosion, the chemical elements hydrogen and helium were made. These elements became the building blocks for the stars in all the galaxies. Although there are other theories, most astronomers accept this model as the basis for further studies.

THE FATE OF THE UNIVERSE

Given that the universe has been expanding for fifteen thousand million years or thereabouts, the question arises as to whether the expansion will continue for ever, or whether the gravitational attraction between all the matter in clusters and superclusters of galaxies (and elsewhere) is sufficient to halt the expansion. The present rate of expansion and the observed average density of matter in the universe point to continued expansion. The average density needed to 'close' the universe and reverse the expansion is equivalent to one house brick in each cube of space with sides 500 000 kilometres long. This does not seem much, but the matter we can see does not quite spread this thickly. However, the observed value is sufficiently close to the critical value that there may be enough cold, dark matter which we cannot see (because it does not shine) to bring the galaxies rushing together into a 'Big Crunch'. Then there may be another Big Bang, and . . .

SUGGESTION FOR A PROJECT

1 Find out about the *steady-state theory* of the origin of the universe.

QUESTIONS

1 List three types of galaxy shape used by Hubble in his classification.

2 Identify the galaxy type for galaxies A, B and C from the following information on their content.

	Old stars	Young stars
A	Many	None
B	Some	Some
C	Few	Many

3 Explain, in simple terms, *how* observations of supergiant stars, bright nebulae and supernovae can be used to estimate the distance to galaxies.

4 What, if any, is the connection between the apparent change in the note of a motor car engine as it passes by at constant speed, and the red shift of galaxies?

INFLATION

The discovery by Penzias and Wilson in 1965 that the universe is bathed in radio waves, which appear to be the 'echo' of the Big Bang in an expanding universe, gave added weight to the hot Big Bang theory. Recent developments suggest that the early universe underwent a period of extremely rapid expansion: these *inflationary* theories go some way towards pushing our understanding closer to the Big Bang. In turn, this suggests the possibility that the laws of physics may be able to explain how the universe came into existence, perhaps out of absolutely nothing!

GALAXY FORMATION

There is a chicken and egg problem regarding galaxy formation. Did the hydrogen and helium produced in the Big Bang form stars, which then assembled into galaxies, or did galaxy-sized clumps of matter arise which subsequently turned into stars? Such clumps, protogalaxies, are part of current theories on galaxy formation, and if they are observable may well have red shifts of between 6 and 25. The current differences between elliptical, spiral and irregular galaxies could be due to the varying rotational velocity of protogalaxies, together with local conditions such as the prevailing magnetic field.

ACTIVE GALAXIES

The quasars can be thought of as one extreme in a sequence of galactic activity, beginning with youthful extravagance and ending in middle-aged moderation. Our Milky Way galaxy is not particularly active.

Assuming quasars to be very distant, the immense energy output comes from a small source. This could be an active black hole, siphoning material from the galactic core. If so, it should become less active as its size increases with age, until the power supply eventually switches itself off (Figure 7.4). Our Galaxy may have a quiet, ageing black hole at its centre. Although hidden from view by interstellar gas and dust, active infra-red and radio sources have been identified there.

Figure 7.4

As a black hole at the centre of a galaxy increases in size with age, matter can fall in without reaching high velocities and high temperatures. Each stage in the sequence could represent the varying degrees of observed galactic activity, from energetic young quasars to normal spirals and ellipticals

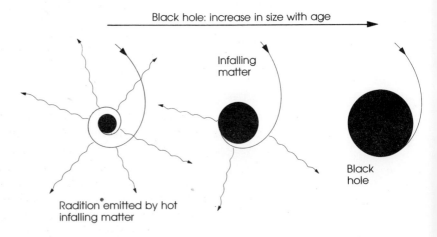

Black hole: increase in size with age

Infalling matter

Black hole

Radiation emitted by hot infalling matter

INTERACTING GALAXIES

Many galaxies are seen which look as though they are undergoing collisions, or are entering or leaving the scene of one. Their peculiar shapes (Figures 7.5 and 7.6) can be explained in terms of the gravitational effect of each galaxy on the other. We see one instant of the event; 'news' of the final outcome will take many millions of years to reach us.

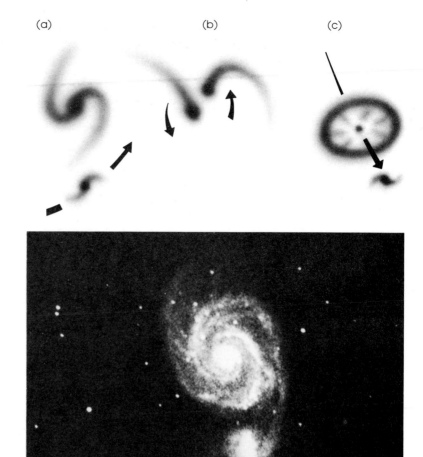

Figure 7.5

The outcome of a galactic 'collision' depends on the mass of the participants and the nature of the encounter. Near misses can produce (a) 'sprung' spirals and (b) 'rat-tail' galaxies. (c) 'Ring' galaxies are produced by the passage of one small galaxy through another; the ring structure is temporary

(a)   (b)   (c)

Figure 7.6

The Whirlpool Galaxy in the constellation of the Hunting Dogs

THE HUBBLE LAW

The red shift (z) of a galaxy, measured by the shift in wavelength $\delta\gamma$ of a spectral line, is found from the equation:

$$z = \frac{\delta\lambda}{\lambda} = \frac{v}{c}$$

where λ is the normal 'at rest' wavelength, v is the velocity of recession and c the speed of light. A red shift greater than 1 seems to imply that the object is moving away at faster than light speed, but Einstein's special relativity theory tells us that matter cannot be accelerated to reach or exceed light speed. There must be another explanation – which is provided by the same theory! As the relative velocity of two galaxies approaches the speed of light, a new formula must be used which 'allows' values of z above 1.

Hubble's law relates the velocity of recession (v) to the distance (d) of the galaxy:

$v = Hd$ (H is Hubble's constant, presently thought to be around 55 kilometres per second per million parsecs (Mpc)).

The faster the velocity of recession, the further away a galaxy is, unless there is another important contribution to the red shift apart from the Doppler effect. One possibility is that red shifts depend on the *age* of the matter emitting the light, so in this scheme quasars could be nearby if they represent 'young' matter which has recently been created. The quasar–galaxy associations could also be accounted for if quasars are created within galaxies, then ejected. Not many astronomers support this theory, but it cannot be rejected out of hand. Whatever the nature of quasars, they will be the subject of intense study for the foreseeable future.

SUGGESTION FOR A PROJECT

2 Using star charts for guidance, observe as many galaxies as you can with whatever optical equipment you have. Try M31, M33, M51, M82, M83, M87. If you use a large telescope, sketch each object.

QUESTIONS

5 Observations of a galaxy show that stars at X have a lower red shift than stars at A, while stars at Y have a higher red shift. What does this tell you about the motion of the galaxy? (It is viewed from Earth at an oblique angle.)

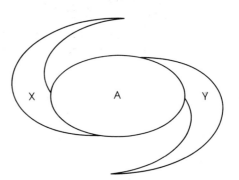

6 A star in the Large Magellanic Cloud (LMC) is known to have an absolute magnitude $M = 1.4$, and apparent magnitude $m = 20.2$. Use the formula

$$M = m + 5 - 5\log_{10}d$$

to find the distance d in parsecs to the LMC.

7 A galaxy shows a spectral shift of 1.5 nanometres (nm) (1 nm $= 1 \times 10^{-9}$ metres) at a wavelength of 400 nanometres.
(a) What is the red shift z?
(b) What is the galaxy's velocity of recession ($c = 3 \times 10^8$ metres per second)?

8 Taking the Hubble constant to be 55 km/s/Mpc, calculate the distance to a cluster of galaxies with red shift $z = 0.03$ (c is given in question 7).

CHAPTER 8

THE CELESTIAL SPHERE

Ancient stargazers believed the Earth to be surrounded by an invisible crystal sphere carrying the stars. We no longer believe in crystal spheres, but in many ways the idea is still useful. If you imagine the Earth to be a table tennis ball placed at the centre of a football, then the inside skin of the football represents the celestial sphere.

HEMISPHERES

Just as the Earth's equator divides our globe into two hemispheres, so the night sky is divided into two hemispheres. Moving a reasonable distance north or south from one terrestrial hemisphere to the other will allow an astronomer to see 'new' constellations which were previously hidden below the horizon at all times. In addition, star patterns visible from both hemispheres on Earth will seem to be upside-down in one relative to the other (Figure 8.1).

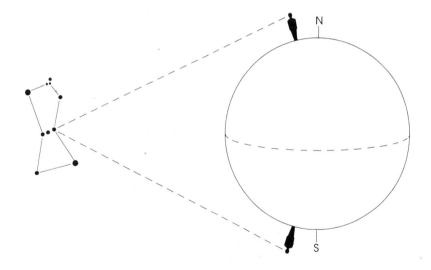

Figure 8.1

The constellation Orion (the Hunter) as seen from each hemisphere on Earth

Pole stars

A line drawn through the Earth's axis of rotation and extended seems to 'meet' the sky of the northern hemisphere at the *north celestial pole* near the star named Polaris in Ursa Minor (the Little Bear). This star is quite bright, and can be found in the sky using two brighter stars in Ursa Major (the Great Bear or

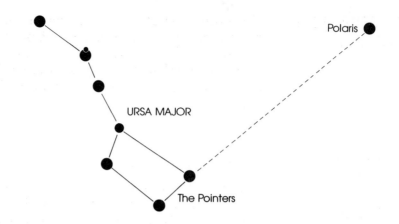

Figure 8.2

How to use 'the
Pointers' in Ursa
Major to locate
Polaris

Polaris

URSA MAJOR

The Pointers

Plough) as shown in Figure 8.2. From Britain the stars of Ursa
Major never dip below the horizon and can be seen whenever
the sky is clear and sufficiently dark.

In the southern hemisphere, the south celestial pole is marked
by a fainter star called Sigma Octantis, which is more difficult to
find than its northern counterpart.

Angles on the sky

If you imagine a protractor as just fitting under the celestial
sphere, you will see that moving from the horizon to the point
directly overhead (the *zenith*) and on again to the horizon
involves turning through an angle of 180 degrees. Astronomers
use the angle between two points in the sky as a means of fixing
positions, and for measuring the 'distance' between objects. For
example, the Pointers in Ursa Major are separated by about 5
degrees, while the Sun and Moon cover only $\frac{1}{2}$ degree from one
side to the other (Figure 8.3).

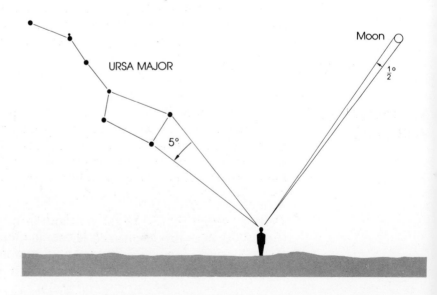

Moon

URSA MAJOR

$\frac{1}{2}^\circ$

Figure 8.3

Angular measure in
the sky. Approximately
ten full moons could
fit between the
pointers in Ursa
Major

5°

CELESTIAL POLES AND LATITUDE

The altitude (height above the horizon in degrees) of the celestial pole is the same as the observer's latitude. Thus from London, latitude approximately $51\frac{1}{2}$ degrees north, the altitude of the north celestial pole is $51\frac{1}{2}$ degrees; from Cape Town, latitude 34 degrees south, the altitude of the south celestial pole is 34 degrees.

ACTIVITY 7

Estimating latitude

Estimate your latitude by measuring the approximate altitude of the celestial pole as indicated by Polaris or Sigma Octantis. A protractor and plumb line can be used as shown in the diagram below.

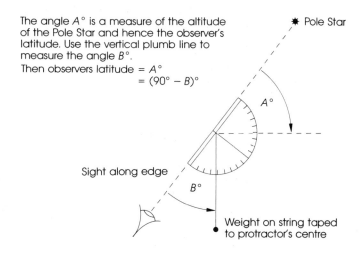

The angle $A°$ is a measure of the altitude of the Pole Star and hence the observer's latitude. Use the vertical plumb line to measure the angle $B°$.
Then observers latitude = $A°$
= $(90° - B)°$

Pole Star

$A°$

Sight along edge

$B°$

Weight on string taped to protractor's centre

STAR CHARTS

When plotted on a map or star chart, the constellations seem very small. Remember, though, that on the sky these same constellations will appear much larger. Recognising them will become easier with experience – once you have located one, you will know what to expect of others, in terms of size and location.

THE CELESTIAL EQUATOR

The projection of the Earth's equator onto the celestial sphere is called the *celestial equator*. Because the plane containing the Earth's equator is inclined to its orbital plane by $23\frac{1}{2}$ degrees, the angle between the apparent yearly path of the Sun against the stars (the ecliptic) and the celestial equator is also $23\frac{1}{2}$ degrees (see Figure 8.4, on the next page).

Twice a year the Sun crosses the celestial equator, once moving from south to north around 21 March and once moving from north to south around 22 September. On these dates, known as the *equinoxes*, day and night have equal length.

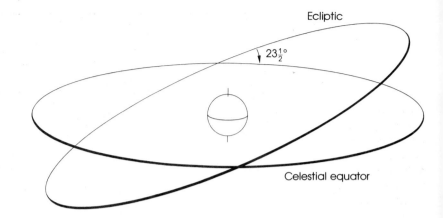

Ecliptic

$23\frac{1}{2}°$

Celestial equator

Figure 8.4

The celestial equator and the ecliptic. As the planets orbit the Sun in the same plane, to a reasonable approximation (Pluto excepted) they are also found on or near the ecliptic

The Sun reaches its northernmost and southermost points at the *solstices*. In the northern hemisphere, the summer solstice occurs in June and the winter solstice in December (see Precession).

RIGHT ASCENSION

The angular distance of a celestial object from the position of the vernal (March) equinox (also known as the First Point of Aries) measured westward is known as the *right ascension* of the object. Abbreviated to RA, or the Greek letter alpha, it is usually quoted in hours, minutes and seconds of time. As it rises and sets due to the Earth's rotation, the First Point of Aries must reach its highest point in the sky (*culmination*) once every 24 hours. The right ascension of a celestial object is the time between the culmination of the First Point of Aries and the culmination of the object in question.

DECLINATION

Declination (abbreviated dec.) is the term used to describe the angular distance of a celestial object north or south of the celestial equator. The declination of the north celestial pole is 90°N (ninety degrees north) or +90°, while anything *on* the celestial equator has zero declination.

Used together, right ascension and declination form a coordinate system which can be used to describe the location of any object on the celestial sphere. Grids showing each are often marked on star charts. In this (or any other) system, the positions of the planets change rapidly due to their motion and proximity, while precession gives rise to slow changes in the right ascension and declination of stars.

PRECESSION

As a result of the Earth moving in the manner of a spinning top (or gyroscope) which is running down, the Earth's rotational axis traces out circles on the sky. The celestial poles move round these circles in a period of 25 800 years (Figure 8.5).

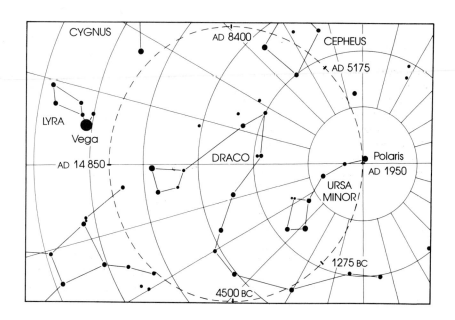

Figure 8.5

The effect of precession, caused by the Moon and Sun pulling on the Earth's equatorial bulge, causes the north celestial pole to trace out circles on the sky

At the moment, the north celestial pole is approximately marked by Polaris, but in the year AD 12 000 this position will be near the brilliant star Vega in the constellation Lyra – as a result of precession.

AN UNEARTHLY VIEW

It can be difficult to appreciate the relationship between terms like celestial equator, ecliptic and precession because of our 'inside' view, which is also limited in time to a few tens of years at most. Figure 8.6 shows these relationships from an unusual vantage point outside the celestial sphere.

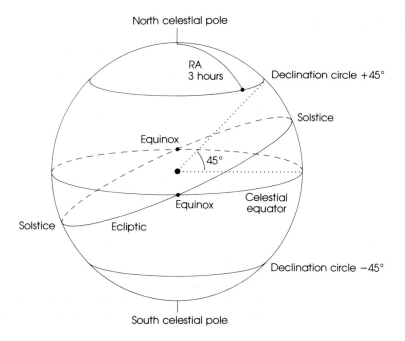

Figure 8.6

The celestial sphere

1 Using star charts and/or the Moon, estimate the angle on the sky equal to (a) the width of your little finger, and (b) the width of your clenched fist, when held at arm's length.

2 Spin a gyroscope to show how the axis of rotation precesses as the rotation slows down.

3 Take a long exposure photograph of a portion of the celestial equator to show the star trails in each hemisphere curving in opposite directions. Use a stationary camera on a tripod, a cable release, and an exposure of at least one hour. Medium to slow speed (100–200 ASA/ISO) film should be used.

QUESTIONS

1 Explain why the constellation of the Southern Cross is permanently out of view from Britain.

2 If the diameters of Earth and Moon are taken to be 12 800 kilometres (8000 miles) and 3200 kilometres (200 miles) respectively, what would be the angular size of the 'full' Earth as seen from the Moon?

3 Sketch the celestial sphere, labelling the celestial poles, celestial equator, ecliptic and a star with coordinates RA 6h 0m 0s, dec. +45°.

4 What is the most southerly declination a star can have to remain visible from latitude 52 degrees north?

5 What are the right ascension and declination of the Sun at the solstices?

6 What is the limiting declination for a star to be *circumpolar* from latitude 52° N?

CROSSWORD ON THE CELESTIAL SPHERE

First trace this grid on to a piece of paper (or photocopy this page – teachers, please see note at the front of the book). Then fill in the answers. Do not write on this page.

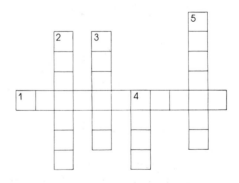

1 Small circular star chart (11)
2 Divides the Earth into two hemispheres (7)

3 The point directly overhead (6)
4 North or South (4)
5 Star in Ursa Minor (7)

IMAGES FROM SPACE

INFORMATION FROM SPACE

The universe is currently sending us all the information needed to unravel most if its mysteries; our problems lie in intercepting the signals and interpreting them. After many thousands of years of naked-eye astronomy, the use of telescopes brought a multitude of new discoveries and theories to explain them.

TELESCOPES

Many objects in the night sky (apart from stars) are invisible unless you use binoculars or a telescope. These instruments use a lens or mirror to collect more light for the eye, and enable you to detect faint objects and to see more detail in bright ones.

ACTIVITY 8

Lenses

You will need a ray box, access to lenses, white paper, a pencil, a half-metre rule, some plasticine to support the lens.

Using a ray box fitted with slits, or another source of illumination, look at the effect of a variety of lenses on two parallel rays of light.

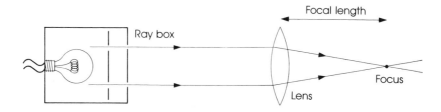

Stand the equipment on a sheet of white paper to trace the paths of the rays as they emerge from the lens. Some types *converge* the rays as shown in the diagram; for these, note how the *focal length* varies as the shape of the lens changes. These and *diverging* lenses can be used in telescopes.

The refractor

This type of telescope uses an *objective lens* to collect and focus light into an image. One of the first refractors was made by the Dutch optician Hans Lippershey around 1608. When he heard of this device, the Italian professor of mathematics, Galileo Galilei decided to make one for himself. Fortunately he had the good sense to point his improved version at the sky. The sights, even in a poor telescope, must have been astonishing – they still are: craters on the Moon, stars in the Milky Way, planets showing phases like the Moon; Jupiter was found to have four moons (the 'Galilean satellites'), which changed their position from night to night as they moved in orbit around the giant planet. You can repeat these fascinating observations with a simple telescope.

ACTIVITY 9

Making a telescope

You will need: a convex (converging) lens of 50 centimetres focal length, a concave (diverging) lens of 10 centimetres focal length, a metre rule, some plasticine.

Place the convex lens 40 centimetres from the end of the rule, fixing it in place with plasticine so that the rule can be moved without the lens falling off. Place the concave lens at the end of the rule nearer the first lens, using plasticine to fix it in place.

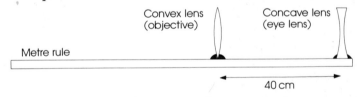

Before using the telescope, make sure the lenses are held firmly in place. Try looking at some objects at a range of distances, moving the convex lens slightly to improve focus if necessary. You may also need to experiment to find the best viewing position by moving your eye towards and away from the concave lens. This type of telescope is similar to the one used by Galileo. Try repeating his observations of the Moon and Jupiter if they are well placed for observation. Do *not* look directly at the Sun with or without a telescope.

ACTIVITY 10

Making a simple modern refractor

You will need the same equipment as that for Activity 9, with a 10 centimetre *convex* eye lens in place of the concave one, and this time place the lenses approximately 60 centimetres apart on the metre rule. How does the view compare with that through the Galilean refractor?

Quality refractors of today use an objective lens made of two components to collect light. This prevents the beautiful but unwanted effect of *dispersion* (Figures 9.1 and 9.2) – when white light is *refracted* as it passes through a lens it splits up into the colours of the rainbow. In a telescope this 'false colour' can make focusing impossible, and the images obtained are useless. Before this discovery, astronomers built extremely long telescopes to minimise the problem.

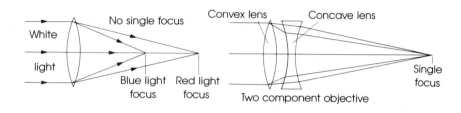

Figure 9.1

The problem of dispersion and its solution

(a)

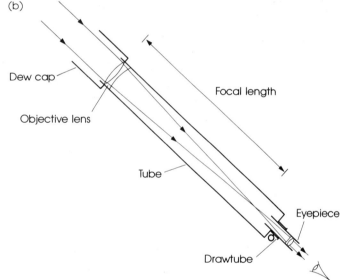

Figure 9.2

(a) A modern astronomical refractor and (b) a diagram showing components

The reflector

A single lens refractor, ancient or modern, is simply not good enough for astronomical use, although in the past astronomers had to go to great lengths to make the best of them. Before the appearance of high quality refractors, mirrors were used to obtain good images from small telescopes. An instrument which uses a mirror to collect light is called a *reflector* (Figure 9.3). There is no false colour in the image, as light of all colours changes direction by the same amount on reflection.

(a)

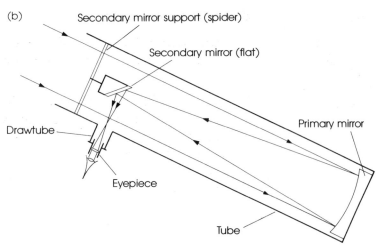

(b)

Secondary mirror support (spider)

Secondary mirror (flat)

Primary mirror

Drawtube

Eyepiece

Tube

Figure 9.3

(a) A reflecting telescope. Note that in this design the observer views from a position at the side of the tube as the light is diverted using a small inclined 'secondary' mirror.
(b) The principal components of a reflector

The first detailed plans for a reflector were published in 1636 by Mersenne. However, it was beyond the technology of the day to construct such a telescope, and little happened until James Gregory revived the reflector with a new design in 1663. Once more it was not possible to build a model which worked well. Sir Isaac Newton produced a simplified version in 1668 using components he had made himself with skill and precision. This worked and gave credibility to the reflector.

Newtonian reflectors remain in widespread use today, together with those of Cassegrain design, in which light is reflected back through a hole in the primary mirror (Figure 9.4).

Mirrors

Initially mirrors were made from an alloy of copper and tin, known as speculum metal, but this changed when glass 'blanks' became available. Modern telescopes use polished glass or similar materials to give an accurate finish, with a surface coating of aluminium to make the mirror reflective. Whatever the material, the precise shape of the surface is important.

Figure 9.4

The Cassegrain reflector

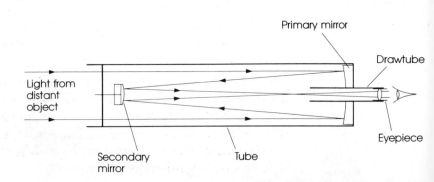

Primary mirror

Drawtube

Light from distant object

Eyepiece

Secondary mirror

Tube

Using spherical mirrors

You will need: a ray box or similar source of illumination, access to small spherical mirrors, white paper, a pencil, a small rule.

Look at the effect of some *concave* mirrors on two parallel rays as shown in the diagram. With only two rays, it will be easy to measure a focal length – try to do the same when six parallel rays are used.

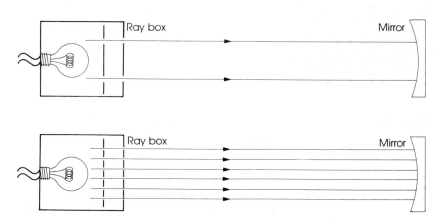

If a mirror is to focus the light from a distant object to a single point, its surface must have a cross-section which is *parabolic* rather than circular (Figure 9.5). The difference between these two curves is slight – a parabolic curve has a slightly deeper centre – but the difference in performance is great. Newton's early reflectors worked as well as they did because the mirrors were almost parabolic.

Figure 9.5

The slight difference between a spherical mirror and one used for astronomical purposes is critical

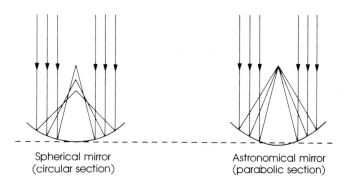

Spherical mirror
(circular section)

Astronomical mirror
(parabolic section)

To show maximum detail in the image, the surface of an astronomical mirror must be smooth and follow the correct shape to within one ten thousandth of a millimetre (about one millionth of an inch). Refractors have lenses made to comparable accuracy, which is why an astronomical telescope is expensive regardless of its type.

Eyepieces: 'What magnification does it give?'

The job of an eyepiece is to magnify the image formed by the object glass or mirror. There is no *single* magnification given, as this depends on the focal lengths of the telescope and eyepiece used. Small focal length eyepieces give high magnifications, but this can be undesirable in small telescopes.

Professional telescopes

The faintest object revealed by a telescope depends on its *aperture*, which is usually equal to the diameter of the lens or mirror. So, to collect more light and thereby see fainter objects, a larger lens or mirror must be used. Unfortunately, large mirrors and lenses distort under their own weight, and this ruins their performance. To date, the largest refractor has an object glass 1 metre (40 inches) in diameter, while the largest reflector which works well has a mirror 5 metres (200 inches) across.

In most circumstances telescope performance is limited by atmospheric conditions. This need not be a question of whether or not it is cloudy. A clear sky can be troublesome if the air is turbulent. A further limitation is *light pollution*; sadly, some observatories are under threat of closure because the sky is so bright through nearby city lights that faint objects can no longer be seen.

Some of the world's largest telescopes

Site	Type of telescope	Aperture
Lowell Observatory, Flagstaff, Arizona	Refractor	0.61 metre
Yerkes Observatory, Wisconsin, USA	Refractor	1.02 metre
McDonald Observatory, Texas, USA	Reflector	2.08 metre
Mount Wilson Observatory, California, USA	Reflector	2.54 metre
Los Muchachos Observatory, La Palma, Canary Islands	Reflector	2.54 metre
Lick Observatory, California, USA	Reflector	3.05 metre
Siding Spring Observatory, New South Wales, Australia	Reflector	3.89 metre
Cerro Tololo Observatory, La Serena, Chile	Reflector	4 metre
Kitt Peak Observatory, Arizona, USA	Reflector	4 metre
Los Muchachos Observatory, La Palma, Canary Is.	Reflector	4.2 metre
Mount Palomar Observatory, California, USA	Reflector	5 metre

Those observatories which produce the best results are situated above much of the atmosphere on high mountain sites, where the skies are frequently clear and dark and the air is steady. The observer's eye has been replaced by photographic film or electronic detectors such as *charge-coupled devices* (CCDs), which are more efficient. Computer control allows astronomers the luxury of remote control from a warm office, which, thanks to satellite communication, need not be in the same country as the telescope.

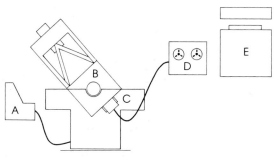

Figure 9.6

A large professional telescope with accessories

A Computer control panel
B Large reflector
C Photographic plate, CCD or spectrograph
D Data storage and processing
E Automated plate measuring machine

INVISIBLE ASTRONOMY

The Earth's atmosphere blocks a lot of the information arriving from space, and our eyes are sensitive to only a small part of the remainder. All forms of *electromagnetic radiation* have the same basic nature as light, but have different *wavelengths*, as shown in Figure 9.7.

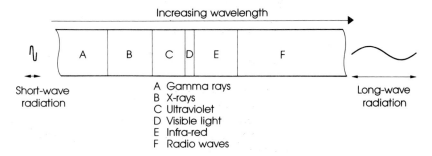

Figure 9.7

The electromagnetic spectrum

Increasing wavelength

Short-wave radiation

A Gamma rays
B X-rays
C Ultraviolet
D Visible light
E Infra-red
F Radio waves

Long-wave radiation

Radiation from each region of the spectrum arrives at the Earth's atmosphere continuously, but only visible light and some radio waves can penetrate easily. Until high altitude observatories and satellites were developed, short 'hops' into the higher regions of the atmosphere using rockets or balloons were used to gather information unavailable at the Earth's surface.

Ultraviolet, X-rays, gamma rays

These short-wave, energetic radiations are harmful to life, so the atmosphere performs a valuable role in blocking them.

Ultraviolet rays from the Sun cause sunburn, and these are emitted by other stars, especially those with a higher surface temperature. X-rays can be detected from the solar corona and other sources (some binary stars) where material is heated to a million degrees Celsius or more. Detecting and focusing these wavelengths is not easy, but they can tell us much about violent events in the universe.

Infra-red and radio waves

These signals have longer wavelengths than light. Both are familiar in everyday events – infra-red lamps are common, and the radiation itself can be felt as warmth from the bars of an electric fire well before they are hot enough to glow. Radio waves with a variety of wavelengths are a major means of communication on Earth, although this can be a nuisance to radio astronomers.

Molecules in space emit infra-red radiation, so telescopes working at these wavelengths can tell us much about the chemistry of the interstellar environment. One particularly successful application has been the study of star formation in dark nebulae, as infra-red can escape whereas visible light cannot.

(a)

(b)

Figure 9.8

Photographs of a nebula in Orion in (a) visible light and (b) infra-red, which reveals more of the nebula's hidden secrets

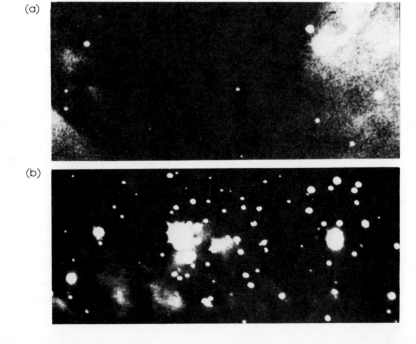

Radio telescopes, such as the Lovell Telescope at Jodrell Bank (Figure 9.9), have the well-known 'dish' shape in most steerable versions and can provide information about objects as diverse as Jupiter, pulsars, quasars and the magnetic fields in space. These sources produce radio waves because of the motion of particles called *electrons*.

Invisible astronomy has led to a number of remarkable discoveries: the existence of pulsars, quasars and starburst galaxies still challenge astronomers to provide explanations. We can now intercept and decode much more of the information arriving from the universe.

(a)

(b)

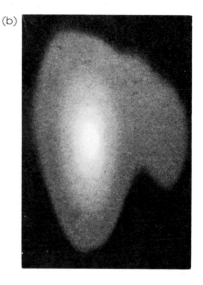

Figure 9.9

(a) The Lovell Telescope and (b) a radio map of a quasar

SUGGESTIONS FOR PROJECTS

1 Make a more sturdy version of a single-lens refractor (see p. 100) by fitting the components in a tube of some kind and use it to study a variety of objects in the sky. If possible, try eye lenses of different focal length and note the change in the images.

2 Find out as much as you can about the following satellites:
   (a) International Ultraviolet Explorer (IUE)
   (b) Infra-red Astronomical Satellite (IRAS)
   (c) Einstein (X-ray)

QUESTIONS

1 (a) Why is it unlikely there will be a refractor larger than 1 metre in aperture in the near future?
   (b) Which telescope accessory provides variable magnification?

107

2 Place the following parts of the electromagnetic spectrum in order of *increasing* wavelength:

Radio, X-ray, Ultraviolet, Infra-red

3 Explain what is meant by light pollution. Discuss the advantages and disadvantages of restricting the amount of street lighting in towns and cities near major observatories.

WORDFINDER ON OBSERVATORIES

Copy the grid below (or photocopy this page – teachers, please see note at the front of the book). Try to find the names of *ten* observatories hidden in the grid. They occur vertically, horizontally and diagonally, forwards and backwards.

B	C	A	U	M	F	A	L	B	P	K	E
D	L	A	N	O	D	C	M	Y	A	R	N
W	O	L	K	U	R	P	E	E	L	G	A
S	I	D	I	N	G	S	P	R	I	N	G
O	C	E	N	T	A	T	O	K	F	W	L
N	A	R	L	W	T	O	Y	E	R	S	K
O	M	D	O	I	P	L	U	S	E	P	C
M	L	E	K	L	M	E	L	O	L	R	I
P	A	R	O	S	E	T	L	E	C	I	L
O	P	A	L	O	M	A	R	T	W	L	R
T	A	L	E	N	O	S	A	F	N	O	E
O	L	O	L	O	T	O	R	R	E	C	L

TELESCOPES: FOCAL RATIO

The distance between the lens or mirror and its focal point (the focal length) can vary for a given aperture. Focal length divided by aperture – in the same units – gives the *focal ratio* of a telescope. For example, a 7.5-centimetre (3-inch) refractor with a focal length of 90 centimetres (36 inches) has a focal ratio of 12, written f/12.

Telescopes with large focal ratio are particularly suited to work which requires a detailed view of small objects – planetary observation, for example. Refractors usually fall into this category. A smaller focal ratio, other things being equal, gives a wider field of view and is more suited for use in observing and photographing nebulae, clusters and galaxies.

MAGNIFICATION

Magnification in a telescope is not fixed, but depends on the ratio of the focal length of the eyepiece used to that of the lens or mirror:

$$\text{Magnification} = \frac{\text{Focal length of the lens or mirror}}{\text{Focal length of the eyepiece used}}$$

Choosing an eyepiece of short focal length will provide high magnification, but this cannot be increased indefinitely. The image in a telescope is similar in some ways to a photograph in a newspaper; enlarge it too much and nothing new can be seen. A rule of thumb regarding the maximum useful magnification is that it should not exceed × 50 for every 2.5 centimetres of aperture.

If a telescope is obtained, it should be equipped with at least three eyepieces to give low, medium and high magnification. For a 15-centimetre (6-inch) aperture Newtonian telescope, suitable eyepieces would give powers of around ×50, ×150 and ×300. Frequently, poor atmospheric conditions will put the maximum *useable* magnification well below the maximum given by the above rule of thumb. If you are observing and find that the image is not sharp when focused, change to a lower magnification.

TELESCOPE MOUNTINGS

The mount used to support a telescope tube assembly during use is very important. It must allow smooth movements yet hold the instrument firmly.

The simplest mounting is the *altazimuth* type (Figure 9.10), in which the telescope can move freely either up and down (in

Figure 9.10

An altazimuth telescope mounting

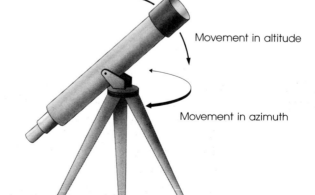

Movement in altitude

Movement in azimuth

*alt*itude) or side-to-side (in *azimuth*). The problem here is that the telescope has to be continually moved in both senses, so that ideally the observer needs three hands – one to adjust in altitude, one in azimuth and the other to focus or make notes. Many telescopes are mounted in this way. One popular variety is the Dobsonian mount (Figure 9.11). It is easy to make and use, but is unsuitable for high magnification and most types of astronomical photography.

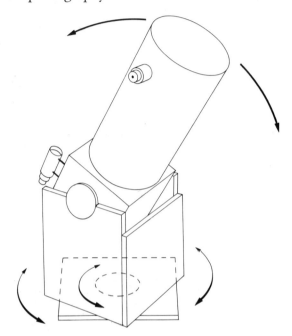

Figure 9.11

The Dobsonian mount – a simple and elegant design

With an *equatorial* mount, one axis is aligned with the Earth's rotational axis by pointing it towards the celestial pole. If the telescope is then aimed at its target and rotated about this 'polar' axis it can counteract the Earth's rotation in just one movement. If a motor is fitted to move the telescope around automatically there is no need for any adjustment at all, provided the polar axis is set properly and the drive rate is accurate.

There are various types of equatorial mount, but they all depend on the same principle. With the German type (Figure 9.12), a second shaft extends at right angles from the polar axis; one side carries the telescope while the other carries a counterweight. In the English type, the telescope is pivoted inside a large yoke, inclined at the correct angle and supported by piers. With a fork equatorial mount, the upper part of the yoke is missing, and the telescope is pivoted between the prongs of the fork (Figure 9.13). All these types have their own advantages and drawbacks; if the telescope has to be moved around, a good altazimuth may be the best choice. For astrophotography and high resolution planetary work an equatorial mount with drive is highly recommended.

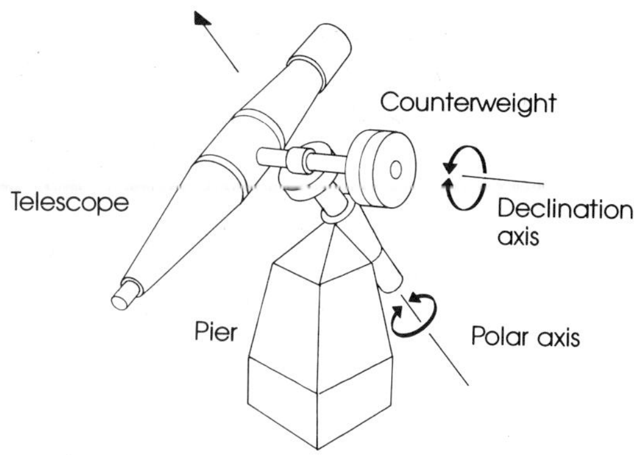

Figure 9.12

A German equatorial mount

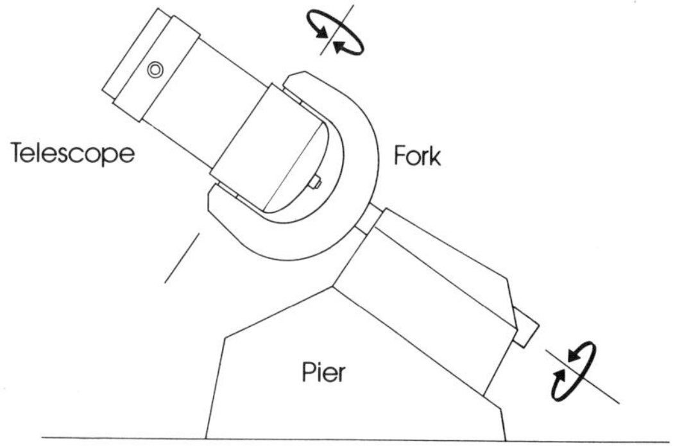

Figure 9.13

A fork equatorial mount

CHOOSING A TELESCOPE

Unfortunately, good astronomical telescopes are expensive. It may be possible to buy a very small instrument for a few tens of pounds, but with poor optics and a flimsy mount, it is bound to be a disappointment to the user.

Telescope performance, other things being equal, is determined by aperture, that is, the diameter of the lens or mirror. It is probably true to say that the minimum aperture for a refractor to be of use for astronomical purposes is 7.5 centimetres (3 inches), while for a Newtonian reflector the lower limit is nearer 15 centimetres (6 inches). When comparing claims, remember that it is aperture (and not some potentially high magnification) which counts.

BINOCULARS

Rather than buy a small telescope, it is better to invest in a good pair of binoculars. Just about any pair will give an improved view of the sky. If the optics are good you should be able to focus stars to pinpoints of light, and the images in each eyepiece should match up. If there is a good deal of false colour, the optics are poor.

If a pair of binoculars is described as 10 × 50, then they give a magnification of 10 and have objective lenses 50 millimetres in diameter. 7 × 50 and 10 × 50 formats are useful; larger binoculars are available but they are costly and difficult to hold steady.

Eyepiece

Prism

Light path

Objective lens

Figure 9.14

Binoculars 'fold' their light path by using prisms to reflect the light beam

THE SCHMIDT CAMERA

Conventional reflectors and refractors provide views of a relatively small area of sky at any one time, a disadvantage when undertaking sky surveys. In addition, the bulk of photographic work is carried out using reflectors with small focal ratios and the images in these instruments lose their quality towards the edge of the field of view. To overcome these limitations, Bernhard Schmidt designed a new type of telescope. By using a large spherical mirror with a short focal length (instead of a paraboloidal one), a *Schmidt camera* (Figure 9.15) can be used to photograph large regions of sky.

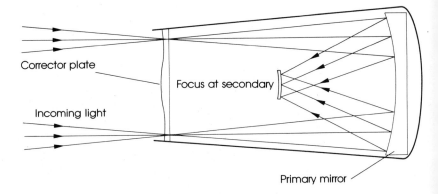

Corrector plate

Focus at secondary

Incoming light

Primary mirror

Figure 9.15

The principles behind the Schmidt camera

Image problems introduced through use of a spherical mirror are corrected using a specially shaped lens (a corrector plate) at the tube opening. The photographic plate is held *inside* the tube in a curve, which results in sharp images across the wide field of view.

ADVANCED TELESCOPE DESIGN

Recently there has been a move away from equatorial mounts for large professional telescopes in favour of the simple altazimuth type. Computer control takes care of the more complicated movements needed to track objects across the sky with this type of mount. Smaller observatories will accommodate such telescopes, giving a further saving in space and cost.

To overcome the problem of very large mirrors flexing under their own weight, new designs are emerging. These use a combination of small mirrors working together, or a mirror made up of many segments (Figure 9.16). Such instruments are in use today and work well as long as their control systems operate efficiently.

There is a telescope in use at Arizona, USA, with six 1.83 metre mirrors linked together. A single mirror 4.5 metres across would be needed to collect the same amount of light. US National Optical Astronomy Observatories advisers are constructing a larger 15-metre 'multiple mirror telescope' (MMT), while the University of California has started work on a 10-metre 'segmented mirror telescope' (SMT).

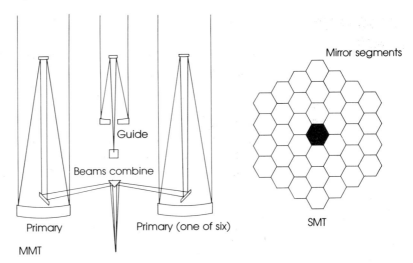

Figure 9.16

The MMT and SMT systems used in modern telescopes

One European scheme proposes to link up four separate 8-metre optical telescopes in an array. This combination will have the same light grasp as a single mirror 16 metres across. The estimated cost: £130 million! Known as the Very Large Telescope (VLT), the array could be operational by 2000.

Active optics

Some of the very latest telescope designs use thin mirrors with hundreds of active supports to counteract flexure. Many times a second, a computer checks the surface of the mirror and sends instructions to the supports to nudge the mirror gently into the correct shape.

FUTURE DEVELOPMENTS: THE SKY'S THE LIMIT

As the size of terrestrial telescopes increases, the limitations posed by the Earth's atmosphere constantly hinder astronomers. Perhaps the most eagerly awaited telescope of all is the *Hubble Space Telescope* (see Chapter 10 p. 118), which will operate in the 1990s.

3 Make models to show the essential features of:
(a) an altazimuth mount
(b) a German equatorial mount.

4 Find out about the 'Haig' or 'Scotch' mount for tracking the stars with a camera and lens. Build a manually-driven Haig camera platform and use it to take long exposure photographs (2–20 minutes) of the constellations.

QUESTIONS

4 What are the advantages and disadvantages of an equatorial mount?

5 A reflector has a mirror 150 millimetres (6 inches) in diameter and a focal length of 600 millimetres (24 inches). What is its focal ratio?

6 What magnification is given by a 10 millimetre (3/8 inch) focal length eyepiece when used with a 200 millimetre (8-inch) f/6 reflector?

7 Why is it not possible to make visual observations with a Schmidt instrument?

8 Is there any limit to the minimum magnification to be used with a particular telescope configuration?

SPACE FLIGHT

The idea of space travel is very old, and the first science fiction novel about flight to the Moon dates from the second century AD, but until modern times it was regarded as nothing more than wild fantasy. It is clearly impossible to use ordinary flying machines for such a journey – the Earth's atmosphere extends upwards for only a very limited distance and aircraft cannot fly in empty space. The only solution available at present is to use a rocket.

ROCKETS

Early scientific papers about rocket flight were published almost a hundred years ago by the great Soviet scientist Konstantin Tsiolkovskii, but it was not until 1926 that Robert Goddard fired the first modern-type rocket, in America.

A rocket works by what Newton termed the principle of reaction (Figure 10.1). In fact, a rocket 'kicks against itself' and can work in empty space. Air is actually a hindrance because it sets up friction and has to be pushed out of the way.

Figure 10.1

The principle behind rocket flight. Hot gases are ejected at high speed, an act which pushes the rocket in the opposite direction

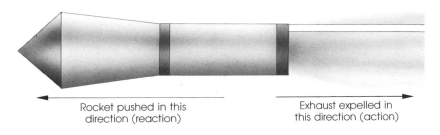

Rocket pushed in this direction (reaction)

Exhaust expelled in this direction (action)

ACTIVITY 12

Demonstrating rocket propulsion

You will need: a small trolley, skateboard or roller skates; a medicine ball or other soft, heavy object. Work in pairs.

Stand (or sit) still on the trolley, skateboard or roller skates, holding a medicine ball. Throw this away to your partner – as you release it, you will move in the opposite direction to the ball. This is how a rocket moves. Swap places and repeat the exercise.

Escaping from Earth

As Tsiolkovskii realised, solid fuels are of limited value, because they are insufficiently powerful or controllable. The solution is to use suitable liquids, a fuel and an oxidiser. These are fed into a combustion chamber where they react and produce hot gases, which in turn escape through the exhaust. A modern rocket motor is very complex, but the principle behind it is simple.

To break free from the Earth, a rocket must work up to escape velocity (11 kilometres per second), but it must do so gradually to avoid being burned away by the heat generated through air resistance. This is why the idea of a space-gun, popularised by the French writer Jules Verne, will not work. Quite apart from the fact that the luckless astronauts would be killed by the shock of departure, they would be burned away before their projectile had left the barrel of the gun.

The atmosphere becomes very thin at high altitude, which reduces the air resistance, but the oxygen in air (which burns the fuel in aeroplanes) runs out. This is why space rockets must carry their own oxidiser.

ROCKET FUELS

Getting into orbit requires an efficient propulsion unit. In order to work well, a propellant must satisfy the following criteria:

- The reaction between fuel and oxidiser must produce a lot of heat.
- The reaction between fuel and oxidiser must be very fast.
- The gases produced by the reaction should have low densities.

The first two points are more easily appreciated than the third, which is investigated in Activity 13.

ACTIVITY 13

Balloon propulsion

You will need: three identical balloons, sources of helium, compressed air, and carbon dioxide. Lung-power can provide the air!

Fill the first balloon with helium, the second with air and the third with carbon dioxide. Try to ensure that each is inflated to the same extent. By inserting a small length of rubber tubing into the neck of each balloon, you will be able to hold them still and make them deflate more slowly so that you can compare the rates of deflation more easily. Once ready, deflate all three balloons at the same time. Which deflates the quickest? Write down the order.

Now refill each as before, tie off the neck and let go (take out the length of tubing first). Place the gases in order of increasing density by noting which balloons float (and which sink) in air.

Returning to the first experiment, can you see how the rate of deflation depends on the density of gas in the balloon?

ARTIFICIAL SATELLITES

The Space Age began on 4 October 1957, when the Soviets launched their first artificial satellite, *Sputnik 1*. It was football-sized, and carried little apart from a transmitter, but it was the forerunner of the important satellites of today. These have all manner of uses: communication, weather forecasting, navigation, assessment of Earth resources and scientific research in weightless conditions, to name but five. Television links over great distances are common today, a feat which would be impossible without satellites. Unfortunately, there are also many satellites launched for military purposes, something which most scientists profoundly regret.

ACTIVITY 14

Observing artificial satellites

On a clear night, an hour or two after dark, look overhead for what appears to be a 'star' moving slowly across the sky. If you succeed in this, you will have found an artificial satellite moving in orbit around the Earth. Some can appear very bright; others vary in brightness as they spin round on their way. In Britain, you can find out when to look for satellites by looking in national newspapers which include satellite predictions.

SATELLITES AND ORBITS

Once launched, the velocity attained by a space vehicle determines the type of orbit it will enter. Many satellites are taken into space by a rocket and then released. If the satellite reaches *orbital velocity*, a circular or elliptical orbit will follow. Needless to say, if *escape velocity* is attained or exceeded, the satellite will be able to escape from the Earth's gravitational field. At the opposite extreme, a very low velocity will result in the craft falling back to Earth (Figure 10.2).

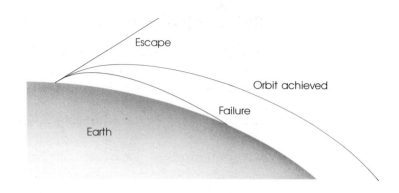

Figure 10.2

The outcome of a
launch depends on
the velocity attained:
giving failure, orbit or
escape

Escape

Orbit achieved

Failure

Earth

Geostationary orbit

Orbiting at 3 kilometres per second at a height of 35 800
kilometres, a satellite would remain over the same point on
the earth's equator. Such an orbit is said to be *geostationary*.
This valuable space corridor is monitored closely to prevent
overcrowding. Other satellites are placed in low orbit, or in a
polar orbit which takes them over the Earth's poles while our
planet rotates below (Figure 10.3).

Figure 10.3

A polar orbiting
satellite

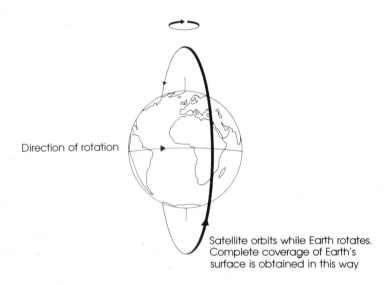

Direction of rotation

Satellite orbits while Earth rotates.
Complete coverage of Earth's
surface is obtained in this way

THE HUBBLE SPACE TELESCOPE

There have been many pioneering satellite observatories in
recent years. A further project, delayed by the *Challenger*
tragedy (see p. 119), will almost certainly provide the answers
to some of the fundamental problems in modern astronomy.
This is the Hubble Space Telescope (HST). Once operational,
the high surface accuracy, 2.4-metre (94-inch) aperture mirror
will be able to detect objects 50 times fainter than the largest
Earth-based instrument. The Hubble Space Telescope
represents a new era of observational astronomy.

SPACE POLLUTION

The threat to missions that do reach the launch pad and beyond will come from the vast amount of space 'junk' already in orbit. Since the launch of *Sputnik 1* in 1957, there have been over 3000 launches resulting in over 3500 objects being placed in Earth orbit. In addition, there are many tens of thousands of pieces of debris floating above the Earth. It would be ironic if the life of the Hubble Space Telescope was ended prematurely because of mistakes already made in polluting the near-Earth environment.

MANNED SPACECRAFT

The first man to fly in space was the Soviet cosmonaut Yuri Gagarin, in April 1961. He was the first to experience a prolonged period of weightlessness. When moving in free fall around the Earth there is no sensation of weight. Weightlessness is harmless over short periods, though the long-term effects have yet to be evaluated.

PROJECT *APOLLO*

In the 1960s the United States government took steps to fulfil one of mankind's oldest dreams, that of walking on the Moon. Through the *Mercury* and *Gemini* missions, America worked its way towards a manned lunar landing. This goal was achieved within the targeted schedule when Neil Armstrong became the first man on the Moon in July 1969 (see Plate 2).

After the success of Apollo, work continued on the other programmes, including *Skylab* and the Space Shuttle. The latter is a delta-wing craft designed for short to moderate journeys into space.

THE SPACE SHUTTLE

NASA's space shuttle is the first re-usable space vehicle. Until the 1981 shuttle launch, other missions had used throw-away machinery. The re-usable orbiter is mounted on a large, expendable fuel tank with two recoverable solid fuel boosters alongside.

The shuttle has been used successfully for scientific, commercial and military payloads and, until the explosion which destroyed the *'Challenger'* orbiter during launch in 1986,

was making space travel seem routine and safe. With the
knowledge gained from this tragic accident, this may be so in
the near future. When the shuttle launches resumed in
September 1988, the possibility that readers of this book
might one day use a similar vehicle for their first journey into
space became more likely.

The Soviet Union unveiled its own version of the space
shuttle in 1988. Similar in appearance to the American vehicle,
the Soviet craft was designed to fly its first three missions
unmanned.

PLANETARY PROBES

It is not possible to send a spacecraft to another planet by the
shortest route. This would involve using power all the time,
and no vehicle could carry enough propellant. Therefore a
probe, sent to observe a planet from close quarters, has to
travel in what is called a 'transfer orbit', coasting for most of
the way. To reach Venus, for example, the probe must use its
rocket motors to slow down relative to the Earth, so that it
swings inward towards the Sun and meets Venus according to
plan (Figure 10.5). Journeys to the outer planets involve
speeding up the space probe relative to the Earth, causing it
to swing outwards. Such journeys take months or years: the
Soviet Mars probes, launched in July 1987, did not arrive
until January 1988.

Figure 10.5

The type of path
followed by a Venus
probe

Orbit to Venus

Earth at
encounter

Venus at
encounter

Sun

Earth at
launch

Venus at
launch

CELESTIAL SLINGSHOTS

One useful procedure is the *gravity-assist* technique, in which
the gravitational pull of a planet is used to accelerate the
probe on to its next target. Thus *Mariner 10* reached Mercury
by way of Venus, and in 1977 the *Voyager* probes were
launched to pass by first Jupiter and then Saturn (Figure
10.6). *Voyager 2* continued on to Uranus in 1986 and reached
Neptune in August 1989. It was fortunate that the giant
planets were suitably placed for such a manoeuvre, a situation
which will not recur for over a century.

Figure 10.6

The gravity-assist
technique was used
to send the *Voyager*
probes to the giant
planets in the manner
of a celestial sling-
shot

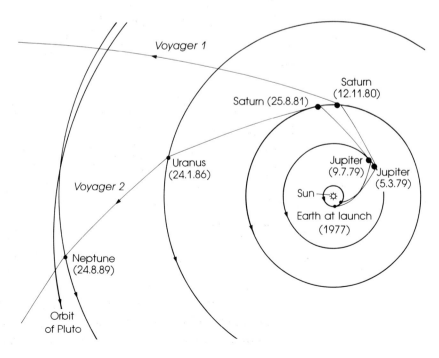

Voyager 1

Saturn
(12.11.80)

Saturn (25.8.81)

Uranus
(24.1.86)

Jupiter
(9.7.79)

Jupiter
(5.3.79)

Voyager 2

Sun

Earth at launch
(1977)

Neptune
(24.8.89)

Orbit
of Pluto

121

FUTURE MISSIONS

Further missions are now in an advanced stage of planning. Among these is a 'Mars rover' which can be moved around the planet's surface, and also a sample-and-return probe to bring back Martian material for analysis. There is also the *Galileo* probe, which will reach Jupiter in the mid-1990s; one section will orbit the planet, while the other will descend into its atmosphere and send back data before being destroyed. The *Cassini* mission will visit another of the gas giants, Saturn.

INTERSTELLAR TRAVEL

Travel to the planets of other stars presents problems of a much greater order. Using today's rockets is out of the question because of the immense distances involved, and futuristic schemes such as 'space-arks' and suspended animation seem likely to remain in the realm of fiction. To achieve such a target, we need a fundamental breakthrough – whether this will come in the foreseeable future, or whether it will come at all, remains to be seen. Until it does, our direct exploration of space must be limited to the Solar System.

SUGGESTIONS FOR PROJECTS

1 Blow up a balloon, release the exhaust suddenly, and note how the balloon moves. Try to harness this rocket-type motion, and build a device which controls the movement. You might like to have a competition, using standard balloons, to build the most efficient balloon rocket.

2 Demonstrate the principle of weightlessness by using a coin placed on top of a falling book.

3 Make a model to demonstrate the flight of *Voyager 2* to the outer planets.

QUESTIONS

1 Give three ways in which artificial satellites have improved. our quality of life.

2 There have been suggestions regarding the launch into orbit of highly reflective satellites, to commemorate important world events. These would become extremely

bright beacons in the night sky. Discuss the implications of this for ground-based astronomy.

3 Write down a list of advantages and disadvantages of working in weightless conditions.

4 Which types of orbit would be most useful for the following satellite applications?
(a) weather forecasting
(b) navigation beacon
(c) telecommunication

5 How would the escape velocity of the Earth change if
(a) the Earth was the same size but less dense?
(b) the Earth's mass was unchanged but the diameter much less?

6 Why should the Hubble Space Telescope outperform telescopes on Earth which are much larger?

7 If a 'sample and return' probe is sent to Mars in the near future, what are the grounds for decontaminating the probe
(a) before launch?
(b) on return?

8 Discuss the arguments for and against continued funding of space research.

APPENDIX I

FURTHER READING

Books

Couper, H and Henbest, N. *The Stars – from Superstition to Supernova* (Pan)
Doherty, P. *Atlas of the Planets* (Hamlyn) (out of print – available from libraries)
Ferris, T. *Galaxies* (Stewart, Tabori and Chang)
Henbest, N. and Marten, M. *The New Astronomy* (Cambridge University Press)
Kaler, J. *Stars and their Spectra* (Cambridge University Press)
Moore, P. (editor) *The Astronomy Encyclopaedia* (Mitchell Beazley)
Moore, P. *Exploring the Night Sky with Binoculars* (Cambridge University Press)
Moore, P. *The Guinness Book of Astronomy* (Guinness)
Moore, P. (editor) *Yearbook of Astronomy* (published annually: Sidgwick & Jackson)
Nicolson, I. *The Sun* (Mitchell Beazley)

Magazines

Astronomy Now (published monthly by Intra Press, Intra House, 193 Uxbridge Road, London W12 9RA)
Spaceflight (published monthly by The British Interplanetary Society, 27–9 South Lambeth Road, London SW8 1SZ)

SOURCES OF SLIDES, VIDEOS, POSTERS

Armagh Planetarium, College Hill, Armagh, Northern Ireland BT61 7HF
Spaceprints, 117a High Street, Norton, Stockton-on-Tees, Cleveland TS20 1AA

NATIONAL ASTRONOMICAL ORGANISATIONS

British Astronomical Association, Burlington House, Piccadilly, London W1V 9AG
Federation of Astronomical Societies (information on local societies): 8 Merestones Drive, The Park, Cheltenham, Glos. GL50 2SS. See also your local library.
Junior Astronomical Society (caters for beginners of all ages) 36 Fairway, Keyworth, Notts. NG12 5DU

APPENDIX II

FORTHCOMING ECLIPSES, AND VISIBILITY OF THE PLANETS

(Note: this is not an exhaustive list.)

Lunar Eclipses visible from Britain

1990 Feb 9 (total) start: 17.30 GMT
1992 Dec 9 (total) start: 22.00 GMT
1994 May 25 (partial) start: 02.39 GMT

Solar Eclipses

1990 July 22 (totality visible from Finland, northern USSR)
1991 Jan 15/16 (totality visible from Australia and
                New Zealand)
1991 July 11 (totality visible from Hawaii, Mexico,
                Central America)
1992 Jan 4/5 (annular – visible from Los Angeles at sunset)
1994 May 10 (annular – visible from Mexico, USA)
1998 Feb 26 (totality visible from Colombia, Venezuela)
1999 Aug 11 (totality visible from England, France, Germany,
                Austria, Hungary, Romania, Turkey, Iran, India)

From locations near to the path of totality a partial eclipse
may be seen.

Visibility of Mercury (evenings, after sunset)

1989 mid- to late December
1990 early to mid-April
     early to mid-August
     early to mid-December
1991 late March to early April
     mid- to late July
     mid- to late November
1992 early to mid-March
     early to mid-July
     late October to early November

Visibility of Venus (evenings)

1989 October to December
1991 May to July

Oppositions of Mars

1990 November
1993 January

Oppositions of Jupiter

1989 December
1991 January
1992 February

Oppositions of Saturn

1990 July
1991 July
1992 August

ANSWERS TO CALCULATIONS

Chapter 1
(p. 13)   Question 12   (a) 5.00 hours (b) 13.00 hours
                          (c) 16.00 hours

Chapter 2
(p. 19)   Question 5   5556 kilometres per hour
(p. 24)   Question 11   100 newtons

Chapter 3
(p. 31)   Question 3   27.2 days

Chapter 4
(p. 55)   Question 15   4 astronomical units (AU)

Chapter 5
(pp. 71–2) Question 6   (b) 1.75
            Question 7   5 parsecs
            Question 9 $3.6 \, M_\odot$

Chapter 6
(p. 83)   Question 7   (a) 40 inches   (b) 4 miles
                          (c) 30 000 miles

Chapter 7

(p. 92)	Question 6	57 500 parsecs
	Question 7	(a) $z = 0.004$
		(b) 1125 kilometres per second
	Question 8	164 000 000 parsecs

Chapter 8

(p. 98)	Question 2	2 degrees
	Question 4	38 degrees south
	Question 6	38 degrees north

Chapter 9

(p. 114)	Question 5	4
	Question 6	120

ANSWERS TO WORDFINDER ON THE SUN

1 Fusion
2 Sunspot
3 Projection
4 Prominence
5 Limb
6 Star
7 Granulation
8 Hydrogen
9 Maunder minimum
10 Moon

ANSWERS TO CROSSWORD ON THE CELESTIAL SPHERE

1 Planisphere
2 Equator
3 Zenith
4 Pole
5 Polaris

ANSWERS TO WORDFINDER ON OBSERVATORIES

1 Mount Wilson
2 McDonald
3 Yerkes
4 Siding Spring
5 Kitt Peak
6 Lick
7 Palomar
8 La Palma
9 Cerro Tololo
10 Lowell

INDEX